STRAIGHT THINKING IN AN AGE OF *Exotic Beliefs*

STRAIGHT THINKING IN AN AGE OF *Exotic Beliefs*

DAN DAY

Pacific Press Publishing Association
Boise, Idaho
Oshawa, Ontario, Canada

Edited by Marvin Moore
Designed by Tim Larson
Cover Photo by Steve Krongard/Image Bank
Type set in 10/12 Century Schoolbook

The author assumes full responsibility for the accuracy of all facts and quotations cited in this book.

Library of Congress Catalog Card Number: 87-42811

ISBN 0-8163-0751-2

87 88 89 90 91 • 5 4 3 2 1

Dedication

To my wife, Brenda, who has always challenged me to use the very principles this book advocates.

Contents

Preface

The title of this book, *Straight Thinking in an Age of Exotic Beliefs,* requires some explanation. It is, perhaps, too bold. The words "straight thinking" infer some standard against which other thinking is being measured. Yet each of the points of view we'll discuss in the following chapters would doubtless claim that its thinking is the most "straight." In this sense, the title of the book may seem presumptuous.

Yet in another way the title may not be bold enough. The issues discussed here have to do with the very basic themes of the Scriptures, and the various belief systems we'll be discussing will be compared against a biblical standard. In this sense "straight thinking" may be too common a phrase, not emphasizing the line between truth and error with sufficiently precise terminology.

However, since this book is written for ordinary people who have an interest in figuring out what's going on in the world, and not for theologians or arcane philosophers, perhaps the title is about right. The intent of the words "straight thinking," as used here, equates them with thinking that lines up with the gospel—with God's remarkable message of salvation provided entirely outside us, which we may receive as a free gift. The standard I'll be applying all through the book is that *ideas or belief systems which interfere with a clear perception of the gospel, however mundane or popular, sacred or secular, are, by definition, contrary to straight thinking.*

In a secondary sense, the emphasis on straight thinking also refers to an effort to bring an element of common sense to the thinking we do about spiritual issues. It is remarkable how clever and creative some of us become, at times, proposing the most circuitous ideas and entertaining the most fantastic conglomerations of supposed theological insights. It boggles the mind how intelligent human beings can actually believe some of it. Yet we do. By the droves.

Why we entertain such "crooked thinking," and how we can escape it, is also part of the book's subject matter.

A Ripe Climate for a Spiritual Emphasis

The signs of the times tell us that we are living in a climate that is ripe for spirituality. Secularity, for all its vaulted claims, has come up bankrupt at meeting the deepest needs of human beings. The glass-and-steel god of technology is turning on us as well, promising answers it cannot deliver and producing a generation of young adults who feel cut off from their spiritual roots, and whose lives are crumbling around them.

As a case in point, during 1987 Americans will spend over $55 billion on cocaine, which has been described as "the most addictive substance ever designed." Unlike earlier drugs, such as heroin and LSD, cocaine is not used just by the down-and-outers of our society or by the experimentally oriented youth. Cocaine hits hardest at the very core of our culture. It is destroying the lives of middle-class men and women at a horrifying rate. An epidemic of drug-related crime, violence, and death is sweeping our nation. The very fiber of our society is threatened, causing *Reader's Digest* to ask in its January 1987 issue, "Can Cocaine Conquer America?"

The need for a return to spiritual values in our culture is increasingly accepted—even, sometimes, in unexpected corners.

In the December 1, 1986, issue of *Forbes* magazine, one of America's leading business publications, Malcolm S. Forbes, editor-in-chief, quoted Sandy McDonnell of McDonnell

Douglas: "Returning to the understanding of and commitment to the basic values of our American heritage in our schools, businesses and government is essential if we are to maintain the freedom that this nation has enjoyed for the last two centuries." Forbes observed, "Teaching and learning about decency, fairness, the Golden Rule, concern for others, the fun and joy of having one's own sense of personal worth, developing an awareness of ethics and morality can be a real turn-on for students and teachers." He went on to call for a return to this value system as our nation's only hope.

Here are two highly esteemed and successful business leaders arguing the case for a return to spiritual values, and doing so in a publication that serves almost as the bible of the business world. Numerous similar examples could be cited, demonstrating the broadening interest in the very values the Christian church espouses.

The climate is ripe for spiritual revival in our society. The question is, What form will that revival take? Will it be a revival sparked by religious forms estranged from the Judeo-Christian tradition? Or will it be one that draws our society back to the arms of a loving God?

Keeping Our Priorities Straight

In light of this growing interest in spiritual values, it certainly makes sense for Christians to consider how well our message relates to the thinking of the secular culture we address. People *are* responsive to spiritual values today—but only as long as those values are made understandable and pragmatic. In other words, we have a tremendous opportunity to show people how applicable the gospel is to the very real human needs that cross every segment of our culture. But in order to take advantage of this opportunity, we need to be sure that what we're saying and how we're saying it makes sense to people who don't have our background. It's a seller's market, but the sellers need to be sure the buyers understand what they're offering.

We understand what we mean in the various ways we

proclaim the gospel, of course. But do others? With all the intramural squabbles that go on inside the Christian community, is it possible that we may become so enmeshed in the intricacies of our own debates that we forget the larger picture? Is it possible for us to get so caught up in who's right about this doctrine or that interpretation of Scripture that the common man can no longer make sense out of it all?

Remaining Sensitive to the Gospel's Potential Consumers

Several years ago I left the pastoral ministry, convinced that what God needed in this world was fewer paid preachers and more laymen with a spiritual perspective. I enjoyed pastoring, and by leaving I wasn't sending a message that I'd lost faith in church organization or pastoral excellence. I just felt *I* could be truer to my convictions doing the very things I'd been telling my parishioners to do—to be God's people *in* the world.

During the past several years I have trained management and sales personnel to think more in terms of the customer or consumer. The central concept which I returned to over and over again, is that if we're not in tune with the needs of those using our services or products, we're always going to be frustrated. But when we begin thinking *like* the customer, the route to satisfying his or her needs becomes clear.

The customers or consumers of the gospel demand this same sensitivity to their needs. If we want to speak to the unchurched, or to those who are in organizations that do not have a clear perception of the gospel, we must understand them. We must bring the focus of the Christian message—the gospel—to the potential consumers with clarity and simplicity. It must make *sense* to them.

Now, the gospel *lends* itself to this. It is simple and clear-cut—a message so beautiful that it is difficult to resist. But we have a tendency to muddy the waters by adding onto the gospel broad conglomerations of our own ideas and practices, creating a confused mishmash that is sometimes overwhelming to the unchurched. We are often so concerned that people not take license with the freedom God allows us that we seek to restrain them with endless qualifications—which results in diluting the clarity of the gospel to such a degree that it almost ceases to be "good news."

When this happens, we're no longer doing "straight thinking." A strong gospel orientation is something we all struggle to maintain. Human nature causes us to seek alternatives to trusting wholly in God, and we all need constant reminders of where our focus should be.

This book is designed to be such a reminder.

Having written several previous books, I know that if you, the reader, don't feel my thinking is "straight" on any of the various issues we'll be considering, you'll let me know. And I welcome that. In the process, perhaps we'll all grow.

While this book is far from perfect, it would not be even as good as it is without the constructive criticism of my wife, Brenda, who repeatedly used the book's theme on me, demanding that the words I was writing make sense in non-theological language. Though I often struggled to maintain my use of the religious jargon preachers are so used to, I realized that her demands for a simple, common-sense approach were appropriate. It's a discipline I suspect all of us who write could use more of.

Introduction

Remember the "good old days," when men were men and the world made sense? When *straight* meant "honest" and *gay* meant "happy"? When everybody who wanted a job had one? When nobody called disciplining children "child abuse," and people loved their families too much to cause them pain? When everybody went to prayer meeting, even when the preacher was boring, and all the churches were full? Did you ever wish the "good old days" were back?

Maybe those days weren't really as good as they seem in memory, but my recollection is that they were a good bit simpler than what we're experiencing today. We are clearly living in one of the most complex periods of our planet's history. Everything that's not nailed down seems to be moving around. Political, economic, social, and religious certainties are all up for grabs.

There are many names that have been given to our age in an effort to explain the rapid pace of change evident in all aspects of life—as well as the repercussions this pace has on us. Futurist author Alvin Toffler speaks of it as the post-industrial age and has coined the phrase, "future shock," to identify the impact these rapid changes are having on individuals and institutions. The future is coming at us all too fast, and in the process is creating major personal and social confusion.

Not Even the Church Has Escaped Being Changed

The Christian church is one very conservative institution which has experienced dramatic changes during this age. The old division into Protestant and Catholic segments is almost obsolete. Protestantism, for example, has splintered into numerous denominational subgroups and new "isms," such as Neo-Pentecostalism, which operates as a type of mega-denomination within Protestant *and* Catholic fellowships. Even mainline denominations, such as Lutherans and Southern Baptists, find themselves locked in heated debates within their organizational structure over matters relating to more conservative versus modernistic viewpoints on the meaning of Scripture.

A weekend review of television preachers creates in microcosm a picture of what's happening in the church. There are pedantic lecturers, whose gentle sermons are accompanied by soft music sung by choirs of fresh-faced young people sitting among trees and beside lakes, their saccharine smiles almost unbelievably strained. There are the screamers and shouters, whose piercing glance and formidable certainty about their beliefs creates an almost manic atmosphere that wrings out the audience and causes a sigh of relief when the program ends. There are the healers, both direct and more subtle, whose message of a spiritual "quick fix" occasionally seems strangely out of tune with the gospel's call for patience and promises for the hereafter. And there are the political activists whose vast plans and strategies to turn America into a Christian nation sound as promising as Judas's similar proposals must have sounded to the disciples during Jesus' day—and which may be just as misguided.

Every viewpoint, it seems, has a televised advocate. It sometimes seems that these modern-day hucksters spend more time pointing fingers at one another—and anyone else with the audacity to disagree with them—than spreading the gospel.

In the face of all this, it's no wonder that many *believers* are confused. Neither is it any wonder that others who might *be-*

come believers hold back, uncertain which way to turn in making a commitment or whom to trust for realizing the spiritual urges they feel.

The Struggle to Make Sense of It All

Because we're all different, coming from different backgrounds with different perspectives on life, it's impossible to create a model of the normal Christian life to which we could *all* subscribe in every detail. There needs to be room for us to be ourselves. A pluralistic spiritual environment allows each of us to hold our own viewpoints on a wide scope of collateral issues, while continuing to fellowship as brothers and sisters in Christ, with general agreement on the *key* issues.

Not all theological issues are of equal importance, nor is it really necessary for us to have total agreement. Still, there needs to be some structure to the approaches we embrace—a basic common ground which allows us to make sense out of all the change taking place around us. Too acute a diversity of opinion, even when it's in the name of freedom to follow our own perceptions of truth, makes us uncertain and stressed. We feel cut off from a sure foundation.

For most Christians, the Bible provides that agreed-upon foundation. While there are many differences of opinion about the biblical text, as well as about specific aspects of interpreting it, it's still the accepted Word of God for the Christian world. The struggle to make sense of the confusion in the religious community, as well as in the world in general, finds common ground in the Bible.

Most Christians agree on the broad sweep of biblical teaching. We agree that Jesus came to show us what the Father is like and to die so those who have faith in Him can live. We may give even these basics our own preferred slant, but we all agree that the Bible was written and perserved so that we could better understand God's intent in relationship to man.

Part of the problem with the many interpretations which spring up once we leave this basic theological territory is that we become so obsessed with peripheral issues that they obscure our understanding of the basics. We get so trapped in the exotic that we lose sight of the fundamental. We continue to mouth our belief in these truths, but our preoccupation with the creative touches our denomination or group has introduced gets between us and the peace we should have from the clear, simple gospel message.

In recent years (with Jonestown and the Charles Manson cult as only two of the most vivid examples) we've had dramatic evidence of the extremes people can go to when they allow rigid, tunneled thinking to control their commitment. Even in the average Christian congregation it is possible to see very un-Christian behavior carried out in the name of Christ. The people doing these things often feel a sense of righteousness because they're obeying a specific dictate of their faith. Yet in the process, they're missing the whole point: God's church is a family of people dedicated to loving as God loved—openly and generously. Christians are supposed to be *good* people. We're not called to change the world. That's God work. We're called to be kind, loving, and accepting. We're supposed to be living examples of how the gospel transforms.

But, too often, we're not.

It All Starts With Jesus

Everything about the Christian religion begins with the person Jesus of Nazareth. The Jesus described in the Bible was a man filled with compassion for the human situation. He's been painted as a revolutionary by some, while others have turned Him into a meek and mild ascetic. The fact is Jesus loved people. The Bible places Him often at parties, weddings, and other joyous social gatherings. Many of His stories were filled with a gentle humor and convivial spirit. He sought out individuals who were outcasts of the community and shared precious moments with them. He mixed as casually with those who didn't fit into the social register as with those who headed it.

There is a calm, common-sense welcome about Jesus. Although He was bringing the most important message the world could ever know, He wasn't a radical. When He dealt with serious error in the picture the religious leaders of His day were painting of God, His rebukes were serious, but not fanatical. Fire didn't come out of His mouth when He reproved sin. Children didn't run from Him, but came to sit on His lap while He spoke.

This image, if we spent time thinking about it, should have a profound impact on the attitude we take toward the religion that has evolved out of Jesus' ministry. Yet sometimes we don't seem to have let this happen. It is sometimes a little difficult, today, to see Jesus in His church.

"Hey, Wait a Minute, Guys"

Have you ever felt that things were getting out of hand? That maybe our world is getting a little bizarre? That people are becoming so wrapped up in "isms" that they forget to consider whether the exotic ideas they're toying with hold up to the simplest questions, such as, "Will this make you a better person?" or "Are you really happy like this?" or "Have you considered all the repercussions of this decision?"

I'm persuaded that there is room for a common-sense look at the Christian world that does little more than say, "Hey, wait a minute, guys. Does all this really make sense? Aren't we getting a little strange, here?" Rarely are we able to get people to change their minds, even when we show them that what they believe is quite preposterous. Still, there is great value in asking these common-sense questions about the belief systems we see all around us, even if nobody's listening to common sense anymore.

After all is said and done, that's what this book is about.

The following chapters will examine a few of the more prevalent exotic varieties of individual and group expression. They are not an exhaustive study, filled with footnotes, quotations, comparative lists, and appendices. Instead, we're going to employ a more popular approach. If you finish the book with a slightly stronger sense of how to relate to the wide

diversity of viewpoints available today, I will feel satisfied.
I hope you will too.

An Overview

The first chapter deserves special attention. What you'll read there may seem obvious, but it's basic to everything else we'll be doing. It presents some common-sense guidelines to Bible study. How we arrive at an understanding of biblical thought is a critical issue that divides Christians—and it's the point where coming together must begin.

If we all agree that the Bible is the basis for our religion, then we need a common understanding of the basic approaches to utilizing it. Among the various exotic belief systems we'll be reviewing, nothing is more characteristic than the disparate ways different ones use the Bible to support their beliefs. This is a theme to which we'll come back over and over throughout the book. You cannot come out with a common-sense view of God and man unless you apply some common-sense guidelines to your use of the Bible.

The concepts we'll explore in this first chapter are not intended as a comprehensive program for Bible study. They are merely an examination of a few of the areas where people seem to get into trouble fairly often—and a few ideas on how to avoid these most common pitfalls. I believe you'll find the ideas to be reasonable and practical.

Succeeding chapters will consider a few of the more common belief systems that compete with mainstream Christianity today. Because of space limitations, none of them will be analyzed in depth. There is danger in this, of course. A surface review can always be accused of characterizations that are inaccurate. Although I cannot be comprehensive in this review, I'll try my best to be fair.

At the end of each chapter there will be a section dedicated to thought questions. If you are merely reading the book through, take a few moments to reflect on them. If you are using the book in a study group, the thought questions will come in handy as a basis for discussion.

In his television program, "The Twilight Zone," Rod Serling used to tell of some ordinary person, living a very ordinary life, until at some point he began to slip away from reality. And we'd hear Serling's narration swell into the words, "Bill and Gladys don't realize it yet . . . but they've just passed into the Twilight Zone." It was, as intended, quite eerie and frightening.

The sad truth is that each day many men and women are passing into the "twilight zone" of spirituality. This book is written in the hope that a little "straight thinking" may help you and me to stay out of the twilight zones of life, redirecting our steps into the *real* world where Jesus lives and dwells as our best Friend.

Chapter 1

Common-Sense Guidelines for Studying Your Bible

"Aw, come on. You can make the Bible say anything you want it to! That's just your opinion."

Have you ever heard anyone say something like that? Have you ever said it or thought it yourself?

Opinion. Interpretation. Truth. How do you know which you're dealing with in any given situation? Everybody has an opinion on what the Bible teaches, it seems. You have an opinion. I have an opinion. Even pastors, theologians, and scholars disagree over the meaning of various passages of Scripture. The simple fact is, we can go through the discipline of learning Hebrew, Aramaic, and Greek, so that we can read the Bible in its original languages; we can study the complex history of Bible translations from the earliest bits of parchment to the latest modern editions—and still have differences of opinion on what the Bible means.

In one way, this is healthy. There should be room for honest minds to disagree and still be friends, shouldn't there? However, as a historical pattern, such differences have proven to be very unhealthful for those who happened to be on the "wrong" side (read: *minority* side). During the Reformation, both Roman Catholics and Protestants became adept at persecuting those who disagreed with them. Protestants from one camp even persecuted Protestants from another—all in the name of what they thought the Bible meant. That same spirit of hostility and bitterness is seen in our day, too, with ringing denunciations and condemnations coming from pulpits and television platforms week after week.

I'm persuaded that a great deal of the confusion and bitterness of the past could have been avoided had believers been willing to bring a few common-sense guidelines to their Bible study. Don't misunderstand me. I'm not trivializing the serious disagreements that have arisen between sincere Christians down through the ages, or even suggesting that the debates have not been useful in arriving at a closer understanding of what God had in mind when He inspired the various writers and compilers of the Bible. But when the apostle Paul counseled young Timothy to study the Scriptures "which have power to make you wise and lead you to salvation through faith in Christ Jesus" (2 Timothy 3:15, NEB) he was emphasizing an important truth: Bible study should lead to wisdom and faith. When it leads to bigotry, hostility, and divisiveness, one must ask what spirit is involved.

We all need to study far more than we do. Yet our study would be considerably more fruitful if we did it with a bit more generosity of spirit and intellectual humility.

The guidelines in this chapter are just that—*guidelines,* not *rules.* Mostly, they are practical suggestions on how to handle the Scriptures faithfully, with a large dose of common sense. They identify some of the more frequent mistakes that developing Bible students make in the way they approach Scripture, and they suggest alternatives. As we approach the Bible, it's important to keep our expectations within reasonable limits. We rarely if ever can determine the absolute meaning of a given passage of Scripture or the single application appropriate for all situations. Even after a lifetime of study, none of us will *know* what the Bible means in every case. All we can hope for is increasing insight. My suspicion is that the more fully we grasp the fullness of God's Word, the more we'll realize how little we actually understand.

Everything else we look at in this book will reflect the concepts we discuss in this chapter. How we handle the Scriptures predisposes us to certain types of theological thinking and practical, everyday behavior. What we believe has a direct and inevitable influence on what we do.

Those who have passed over into the "twilight zone" of ideas have often done so—partially at least—as a reaction to the rigid, cruel, and unforgiving attitudes displayed in the traditional Christian churches. When our own reading of the Scriptures leads us into closed, negative attitudes and behaviors that drive others off, how can we blame them for being confused about God? Aren't we His representatives? Aren't we supposed to show people what *He's* like by what *we're* like?

The reason we're considering this factor here is that the way we behave as Christians usually stems from what we think the Bible teaches. Few of us would say, "Well, the Bible teaches that we should all be loving and compassionate, but I've decided to be a real bigot, treating those who don't see things my way with cruelty and derision." We don't directly disobey God. Instead, we find biblical support for the attitudes and behaviors we elect to display. We take a text here and a text there and combine them to justify our approach to others.

We usually don't do this consciously. We're just reading the Bible *selectively*—clinging to those passages that ring true to what we want to believe and ignoring those that don't. For example, the Old Testament is filled with statements that affirm the loving nature of God and testify to His plan of saving mankind through the gift of His Son, yet the Israelites persisted in trying to work their way to salvation. He sought to establish a covenant of faith, but they demanded a golden calf. He wanted to drive out their enemies before them in the Promised Land, but they persisted in waging war. He wanted them to be a city set on a hill, a beacon light to the surrounding nations, but they built walls and fortifications, keeping the truth to themselves and rejecting all overtures from the Gentile world.

Taking their lead, many of us today continue to use our understanding of biblical truth to shut out the ideas of others. Instead of finding in the Bible the loving God who made overture after overture to lost mankind, we're like Jonah, who sat on the side of a hill waiting for God to destroy the ungodly city of Nineveh, and who even went so far as to lecture God for being more interested in saving lives than in fulfilling the judgments His agent had declared.

Understanding the Bible involves more than reading its words. We must also grasp the larger picture of what God is doing in the world. We must put specific texts and situations into the broad background of God's plan to save the human race. Short of that, our reading of the Bible will always lead us into confusion and loss. What God says is part and parcel with who God is.

Guideline 1: Never study God's Word without asking God's Spirit to guide you.

A prayerful attitude toward the study of the Bible involves more than just tossing up a terse, "Help me to understand Your Word, O Lord," before plunging in. It requires a conscious willingness to be led into deeper understanding, which often means seeing things which run counter to our entrenched opinions.

This is an issue of particular impact for those who already profess some expertise about the Bible, such as pastors, Bible teachers, and church leaders. It's very difficult to approach God's Word with humility when everyone around us is praising us for our insight and depending on us to speak with authority. It is hard, sometimes, to say, "I don't know," or "all I can give you is an opinion." Yet, if we were really honest about it, much of what we proclaim so dogmatically—even from the pulpit—contains more than a little personal opinion.

We all *have* opinions—and have every right to defend them enthusiastically. However, it's when we deceive ourselves into believing our opinions are more than opinion that we get into trouble. We should all stand by our convictions; yet we need to avoid the temptation of playing God. We're all merely mortal humans, struggling to get a clear understanding of what God wants us to know. It never hurts to allow that others' opinions, even when they differ from ours, are possibly true.

God *will* lead us into truth. But we have to be open to being led. Prayer puts us into this willing attitude.

Guideline 2: Organize your schedule to allow a systematic approach to Bible study, and plan a time when you can give it your full attention.

Haphazard study of the Scriptures is little better than no study at all. You've no doubt heard people described as "having just enough information to be dangerous." That's the way we are when we develop sloppy Bible study habits. We *think* we know the Bible, when, in fact, we only know part of the story.

Some people find an hour or so early in the morning before the rest of the family members are up and moving about to be the ideal time for systematic study. Others prefer the hours after the family has gone to bed. The time doesn't matter so much as our commitment to give our study a reasonably uninterrupted segment out of our schedule. We're all busy, with many important tasks to achieve during each day. But if we include God's Word in our schedule, the rest of the day will go easier.

Similarly, the amount of time we spend is no more important than how carefully we spend the time. Quality of time is the key—what we might call a results orientation. We study to grow, to know God better, and to find encouragement. We don't study to "put in our time." However, we need to be honest, not trying to claim we're spending "quality time" when we're just too lazy to invest significant time. It can generally be said that if we spend less than an hour at a time in study, we're probably not providing a segment long enough to achieve any significant insights. There's a difference between garnering an inspirational "thought for the day"—which can take only a moment—and doing real Bible study. And there's a place for both.

A similar issue is the question of getting an overview of the whole Bible, as opposed to focusing our study only on a particular segment. Those who consider themselves "New Testament Christians" sometimes fail to see the value of studying the Old Testament in light of the deeper, more profound teaching provided by Jesus and the apostles. They divide the

Bible into old dispensation theology and new dispensation theology, inferring that the Old Testament teaches a gospel of works, while the New Testament teaches the gospel of grace.

There is a surface appeal to this logic. The New Testament *is* a more obvious presentation of the gospel. Many prophecies about Jesus had been fulfilled *in* Jesus. But it is very difficult to grasp the full meaning of what we read in the New Testament without the strong foundation provided in the Old Testament. Remember that the Bible Jesus used in teaching His disciples about faith and love was the Old Testament. The Bible Paul used to support his majestic theological dissertations on righteousness by faith was the Old Testament. And it was from this Bible that the early church brought to the Gentile world the good news of a Saviour who died to save us from our sins.

It is true that at times the Old Testament seems to suggest a gospel of works. The Jews were always trying to find new ways to work their way into God's favor—as we all do. But the Old Testament doesn't *teach* a gospel of works, in the sense that it was God's plan for people in that era to be trying to work their way into heaven. From Genesis to Malachi, the Old Testament shows God offering salvation through faith in His coming Son. The New Testament itself cites examples from the Old Testament, over and over again, where this is true. The eleventh chapter of Hebrews, in particular, traces in detail the great champions of faith all through the Old Testament.

The God of love is in the Old Testament too.

Rather than trying to read the Bible from beginning to end, many find it useful to be reading in several sections at the same time—in a form of parallel-tracks approach. Try reading from Genesis, the Psalms, and the Gospels as your three starting points. Read each section for a few minutes, then turn to the next, and then the next. During the course of a year, you can probably read through the whole Bible this way, keeping your interest alive through a variety of writing styles and emphases.

Guideline 3: Use a variety of translations in your study, some quite literal and others more interpretive.

Unless we're true biblical scholars, having spent a lifetime handling the original languages in which the Bible was written (and perhaps even then), we need to be careful in assuming we *know* what a passage of Scripture means. The use of many different translations helps us be cautious in asserting specific applications until we can stand firmly on a wide body of biblical teaching and general agreement among translators.

My personal study of biblical languages and textual criticism during college and graduate school was in many ways an exciting, illuminating experience. But what I really learned during it all was how very cautious I need to be about interpreting the Bible—and how very slow to claim expertise. As I spent those many hours studying microfilms of the ancient manuscripts themselves, laboriously translating words, sentences, and paragraphs from those handwritten fragments of skin, cloth, and paper, I acquired a great dose of respect for those who have labored to transmit a fair rendering of the Scriptures for our use today. It was a tougher job than most people realize.

Bible issues are usually far more complex than they seem on the surface, and the dogmatist who pounds the pulpit and proclaims, "My Bible teaches that . . ." had better make sure he's talking about the broad concepts of Scripture that are repeated over and over in different settings. If he's trying to prove too much from a single text, chances are he's in deeper water than he realizes.

There are numerous translations of the Bible available today, and we can usually tell what kind they are by reviewing the introductory material in each. Some, like the New American Standard Bible, strive to give a very literal rendering of the words of Scripture, though they do include some interpretation, since it is impossible to translate without it. Others, like the New English or Phillips versions, are more casual and interpretive—more a paraphrase than a translation. They seek to give some flair to their translations, and in the process introduce more opinion. They are refreshing, but need to be studied with perhaps a little more caution. Still others, such as The Living Bible, are paraphrases. They seek to capture the meaning of passages, rather than depend on the specific words in the original languages. They, too, have value—but should be used more for inspiration than for careful study.

The key is to compare translations of passages in several versions. If you love the majestic language of the King James Version, you're in good company. Millions do. There may never be another translation as beautiful. But when it comes to study, use it in conjunction with several others.

Guideline 4: Assemble some basic study aids to make it easier to develop skill in moving from passage to passage in the Bible.

There is no spiritual merit to be obtained from going blindly into the Scriptures, using intuition as your only source of assistance. Many others before us have also labored to understand the Scriptures better, with the result that a wide variety of very useful study aids has been developed.

The single most valuable tool for systematic study of the Bible is a good concordance, such as *Young's* or *Strong's*. These are bulky books, and they're not cheap. But, if we want to do serious study, it's essential to be able to trace the key concepts in their various applications all through Scripture. You could do it all yourself, comparing word to word laboriously, but the investment of time required can easily become discouraging. There's no reason to reinvent the wheel. So buy a good concordance.

There are also numerous commentaries available that illuminate the meaning of the Bible, from single volumes covering specific books of the Bible to multi-volume sets that cover the whole Bible. These commentaries offer introductory sections on each book of the Bible that explain the historical background of the book, including such matters as who the author was, when he wrote, and what historical factors may have influenced his writing. There is usually also an outline of the book in the introduction, which will help you understand how the various sections relate to one another. These introductory sections are then followed by a verse-by-verse commentary on the book, with insights into the developing message the author was communicating, along with comparisons with similar concepts or wording in other parts of Scripture.

It should be noted, however, that commentaries are, by nature, highly interpretive. What you get in a commentary is somebody's opinion. You'll probably feel most comfortable with a commentary written by a person or group whose theological slant is fairly close to your own.

Keep in mind that it is difficult even for scholars to draw the line between historical fact and the suppositions they draw from it. They write out of their own perceptions about God, His Word, and the Christian life. No commentary is absolutely correct in all places. Still, a good commentary can be very illuminating.

Guideline 5: Before taking a text from one part of Scripture and connecting it with another from a different part, study each passage of Scripture in its context.

There is much to be said for a thematic study of Scripture. It's exciting to see how a passage in one part of the Bible fits with another somewhere else to create a tapestry of truth. It's like doing a term paper, where we gather quotations from famous people in all walks of life to prove a thesis.

The problem, however, is that while it may *seem* that all the passages are talking about the same thing, they may not be.

Studying the Bible in context is the single most important rule for arriving at sound conclusions. And it's the one most often violated. Let's consider a simple example. In 2 Corinthians 9:7 the Bible says, "Each person should give as he has decided for himself; there should be no reluctance, no sense of compulsion; God loves a cheerful giver." NEB. It would be very easy to use this passage as a basis for rejection of any form of systematic giving. Isn't God telling us that we should give according to our *feelings*? However, when we look at the paragraphs before and after this statement, we see that the intent is to place our giving patterns on a surer foundation. The apostle argues that when we realize how much God has given to us, our hearts are touched and we give far more than we ever would have otherwise. Contrary to the "apparent" meaning of this passage (give whatever you please, whenever you are inclined), its true intent is to make us *more* committed and our giving more generous.

It is always important to grasp the *flow* of a section of Scripture and to see how one text leads naturally into the next. The books and letters of the Bible are generally not disjointed "sayings"; they are specific messages, organized according to a logical progression that we need to grasp if we're to arrive at a clear understanding. We would save ourselves a tremendous amount of confusion by applying this one principle to our general study of the Bible. It's not optional. It's essential.

Guideline 6: When in doubt over the meaning of a passage of Scripture, stick with the least exotic interpretation unless there are compelling reasons for doing otherwise.

Have you ever had anyone ask, "Why are you making it so complex? The meaning of that passage is *obvious*." If there is anything that *is* obvious in such a situation, it's that if the two of you are in disagreement, the meaning *isn't* obvious. So don't allow such tactics to deter you from careful study on your own.

Still, it doesn't make sense to reject a simple explanation for the meaning of a passage of Scripture in preference for one that is highly complex and obscure. Some Bible teachers are so clever in the way they find meanings within meanings that the average person feels totally at a loss to figure out *how* he got *what* he got from a given passage. And with cause.

All during His ministry, both in parable and in explicit statements, Jesus warned His disciples that His was not an earthly kingdom and that He would be taken from them in the end, put to death, and then resurrected to establish an eternal kingdom. Yet when He was arrested, the disciples fled in confusion and betrayal. When He was crucified, they collapsed in despair. And when He rose, they refused to believe it. They thought all His words were to be taken in a "spiritual" sense. There wouldn't be any blood. There wouldn't be any cross. There wouldn't be any dirty, sweaty agony. Yet Jesus meant exactly what He said.

It's a good concept to keep in mind. Go for the simple before you resort to the exotic.

Of the several belief systems we'll be examining in succeeding chapters, many refer to the Bible or to Christian literature to support their ideas. Sometimes the most exotic ideas are drawn from passages of Scripture which seem to have nothing at all to do with what they are used to defend. Yet in the minds of those who use these passages, they seem very clear. At the root of this remarkable phenomenon is a basic misunderstanding of how to interpret the Bible. Whenever we quote Scripture out of context, we're in great danger of misusing it.

God's Word deserves better treatment.

Guideline 7: Be Christ-centered or gospel-centered in all your conclusions as to "the real meaning" of passages of Scripture.

As we've just seen, it is so easy to "use" the Bible rather than *listen* to it—to enforce on it our own objectives instead of allowing God to achieve His objectives. The Bible is the revelation of what God has done, is doing, and will do to save us. What God said to Moses on the mountain was said in light of Jesus. What He told the Israelites to do in building the temple was done in light of Jesus. What Paul wrote about Christian behavior was written in light of Jesus. What John outlined in the Revelation was outlined in light of Jesus.

Any focus, other than a Christ-centered focus, distorts the true meaning of the Bible. It's very easy to allow our focus to slip—and it usually happens without our even realizing it has taken place!

Whether the section of Scripture you're studying is in the five books of Moses at the Bible's beginning, or the letters and books of the apostles at its end, you must keep in mind that God is more interested in your eternal salvation than in satisfying your curiosity concerning every aspect of His universe. The Bible isn't a textbook on history, politics, economics, cosmology, or geology. It's a guidebook on how lost men and women can find salvation.

Does this mean that anything the Bible says (or seems to say) about these other topics is incorrect or irrelevant? Not at all. Using guideline 6, in the previous section, we would argue that the preferred approach is the simplest approach—taking what the Scriptures say at face value.

However, if you're trying to use the Bible to argue issues in fields it was not specifically written to illuminate, you're in danger of missing the whole point—and in the process creating controversies you will never be able to resolve until you can sit down with God someday and ask Him about it. These controversies may be interesting and exciting, but they often confuse those listening in who have neither the background nor the spiritual maturity to make sense out of what is being said. Speculative ideas have their place in our lives, but we need to label them for what they are.

When scientists extrapolate far beyond what the data actually prove in order to support a theory, they are misusing their position as thought leaders. The same principle holds true for those handling the Scriptures. We need to know the difference between fact and opinion and be honest in acknowledging when we're speculating.

Guideline 8: Resist the temptation to use your newly won Bible knowledge to clobber others into agreeing with you or doing things your way.

Approaching Scripture with a Christ-centered focus also involves avoiding the temptation to club people over the head with the ideas about life and behavior you've gleaned from reading the Bible. There is an arrogance here that is wholly un-Christian. There's no such thing as a "gospel club." It's either not a club, or it's not the gospel. A mean-spirited Christian is a contradiction in terms.

When the apostle Paul told the Corinthians that a woman shouldn't go to church to pray or prophesy without a shawl over her head (see 1 Corinthians 11:5), was he laying down a rule we should impose on all women in all Christian churches for all time—in short, a club to use against women who don't cover their heads? Few today would argue that this was Paul's intention. Why? Because we understand that Paul was applying the broad objectives of the gospel to a specific situation. In the society of his day, a woman was not considered respectable if she went to worship bareheaded. As a Christian, the woman could have exercised her freedom and gone bareheaded. But Paul didn't want her to hinder her witness by exercising this freedom. His point in this biblical counsel was that saving souls is more important than the clothes we wear or don't wear. He takes the club out of our hands by directing our attention to compassion. We can't use this specific application as an absolute rule because its intent is to make us more sensitive to the needs of others—a *principle* that requires varied applications in varied situations.

This fundamental concern for others is a concept we'd all do well to keep in mind—especially the next time we elect ourselves God's committee of one to "straighten out" someone who doesn't see things just the way we do. Love for people lies at the core of the gospel. If we're arriving at applications of Scripture which do not display compassion and generosity of spirit, we may be *textually* accurate, but we are *contextually* out in left field. Understanding the words of the Bible, but missing its message, is a personal tragedy of immense proportions.

As you use these simple, common-sense guidelines in your study of the Bible, keep in mind that the God who inspired the Scriptures is ever accessible to those who seek to understand. The Bible is not difficult to grasp—it's just that we're not always eager to hear what it is actually saying. A person with an open, teachable spirit, who approaches Bible study with intellectual humility and a desire to discover what God wants to say to him or her, will find the truths of Scripture easy to understand.

Thought Questions:

1. How do you feel about the suggestion that some of us read the Bible "selectively"? Have you ever been guilty of picking and choosing from biblical ideas, casting aside those that didn't fit your preconceived beliefs?
2. In your opinion, what are some of the key factors in determining the best schedule for Bible study? Is there one best schedule for everyone?
3. Which translation of the Bible do you enjoy the most? Why?
4. What is your understanding of the recommendation to study the Bible "in context"? What are the dangers from not doing so? Do you think it really matters?
5. When someone disagrees with your understanding of what the Bible teaches, how does it make you feel? How do you react to people who don't see biblical matters as you do?

Chapter 2

Living in a World of Rampant Secularism

Learning to handle the Scriptures with care is an *internal* essential for Christians. It's not something someone ought to have to tell us to do. If we get off balance at the point of how we use the Scriptures, we're in *basic* trouble. Everything else we believe, teach, or do in the *external* world comes into question. The image we present to the unchurched world can really become distorted.

Yet once we've arrived at a reasonable level of caution in how we use the Scriptures, we've only *begun* the process of interacting with the larger world outside the Christian faith. Now we must come to grips with the fact that there are numerous belief systems competing with ours—systems that are adhered to with just as much sincerity and passion as we display toward the gospel. We miss the point if we look down our noses at those who don't see things our way. The gospel is not a passive message. Neither is it an elitist message, which we can hold to with spiritual snobbery.

We must be able to set our beliefs down alongside the beliefs of others and show how they better meet the needs of men and women in our modern age. In our day, one of the most challenging belief systems against which we must daily compete is secularism, which rejects God or religion as guiding forces in life.

Secularism As an Exotic Belief

Exotic beliefs. They come in a wide variety of forms. It's difficult, perhaps, to think of *secularism* as an exotic belief among all the others we'll be considering throughout this book. Yet if we're to get a sense of perspective on the world views that are in contention with Christianity today we must begin with secularism, which is in many ways the most subtle and dangerous.

Secular humanism lies behind most of the current scientific and technological advances in the Western world. While there are scientists who are Christians, secularism is still the basic "creed" of the scientific community. It is also the accepted educational philosophy in our public schools, taught on all levels, from kindergarten to graduate school. So prevalent is it, in fact, that we don't usually think of secularism as a distinct belief system. We think of it, rather, as the "given," the normal view of life against which all others must be measured. Yet secularism, as a predominant view of the world, didn't even exist until modern times. Today it, too, is a distinct "religion," with a complete set of orthodox beliefs and its share of nearly fanatical believers.

Secularism is a world view that rejects all forms of organized religion save its own and accepts as valid only the facts and influences of the present life. In their book *The Future of Religion,* sociologists Stark and Bainbridge define secularization as the erosion of belief in the supernatural, that is, a loss of faith in the existence of otherworldly forces.

Although secularism didn't exist as a dominant force until the last three centuries, it would be a mistake to assume that there have been secularists only in modern times. There have always been those who discounted the spiritual and sought to live purely on the basis of their own perceptions.

We see the first secularist come on stage in the biblical story of Cain and Abel, as Cain elected to place himself outside of a reference to God. He declared his independence from spiritual involvement by murdering his brother. The process began when Cain brought an offering of fruits and vegetables instead of the required sacrificial lamb. This may seem a small divergence, fully reasonable since he was a farmer. However, by this act he declared that he, not God, was responsible for decision making in all areas of life. And he rejected the gift of salvation that God offered through the sacrificial service, preferring instead the salvation that could be found through his own efforts.

In the years since, and particularly during our present age, secularism has become a complex system with implications for every aspect of life. Any kind of straight thinking in our day must include a consideration of the secularist position.

Philosophical Basics of Secular Humanism

Langdon Gilkey, one of the most widely read theologians of our day, lists in his book *Reaping the Whirlwind* four philosophical premises that characterize secularism:

Contingency. Contingency is the belief that everything that happens is caused by some natural phenomenon in a universe that has always been just as it is today. The contingent aspect of secularism denies the idea that God's hand can be seen in human events. It asserts that our world evolved according to predictable patterns, one event leading to another, and that natural forces have caused all that we see.

Autonomy. Autonomy is the belief that humans came into being by chance and are thus the only ones who can establish the meaning of their lives or chart their ultimate destiny. The idea of accountability to God is totally rejected by the autonomy aspect of secular humanism. As evolved apes, to whom should we feel responsible but ourselves? We are the masters of our own destiny.

Relativity. Relativity is the belief that there are no moral absolutes and that behavior is totally controlled by time and place. If our existence is only a matter of chance, then to speak about right and wrong makes no sense at all. Everything is relative. What's right for one person may be wrong for another. After all, our cultural attitudes toward behavior, both noble and reprehensible, are but the passing view of the current majority. In time, these too will pass.

Temporality. Temporality is the belief that there is no empirical evidence of life beyond the grave and that the world is moving toward its own extinction. The secularist is not necessarily an atheist in the technical sense. He is not *against* God. But he rejects the idea that life beyond the grave can be assumed and holds that spiritual beliefs are without credence unless or until scientifically demonstrated. To him, the world came to be by accidental forces, and in time will cease to be—by the action of those same, uncaring forces. Mankind is merely a momentary bubble of sentience in the flow of oblivion.

Clearly, secular humanism has no place for the transcendent, immanent, knowable God described in the Bible. Carl Sagan, the best-selling author and lecturer, whose public television programs on science have made him into a kind of guru for secular humanism, states the fundamental posture of secularism very simply in his best seller *Cosmos.* He writes, "The cosmos is all that is or ever was or ever will be." On a similar note, Jacques Monod, who was the co-winner of the Nobel Prize for medicine in 1965, states in his book *Chance and Necessity,* "Chance alone is at the source of every innovation, of all creation in the biosphere. Pure chance, absolutely free but blind, is at the very root of the stupendous edifice of evolution."

Mankind: Evolved Animals

Secular humanism has what Christians would consider a very low esteem for the human race. Instead of being God's children, created in His image and destined to dwell with Him, as the Bible describes us, secular humanists see us as merely evolved animals, cousins to the apes, tracing our origins back to river slime, and with the destiny of evolving only until, like the dinosaurs, we are usurped by another order of beings—perhaps the insects, this time.

From this perspective, issues having to do with morality and ethics take on a totally different light. There can be no right and wrong, per se. Instead, there are varying mores dependent on specific circumstances and contemporary views. Everything is relative. As evolved apes, we've learned to behave in ways that allow us to work together—most of the time, but doing so is no more inherently "good" than joining in scavenger packs that wander from one fertile valley to another, beating other tribes over the head with clubs and stealing their women. When we go to war, it's just a technologically advanced version of cave man's rock-throwing conflicts with the mangy pack of humanoids from over the hill.

Going the Full Circle: A Reactionary Response

Interestingly enough, the widespread authoritative stance taken by secular humanism has created a religious backlash. Studies indicate that interest in religion—or at least in spirituality—is on the rise today and that the interest seems to be focused not on the ethical or moralistic aspects, but on those elements that have specifically to do with the supernatural. Stark and Bainbridge state: "What organizational secularization has produced is a large population of unchurched people who retain their acceptance of the existence of the supernatural. They seem only to have lost their faith in the ability of the conventional churches to interpret and serve their belief in the supernatural."

It would be a mistake, however, to infer that secular humanism is on the wane. It continues to be the dominant world view of the Western technocratic structure and is the view our children absorb as they pass through the public school system. Still, the reemergence of an interest in the supernatural suggests opportunities for the gospel.

A Christian Response

Of all the viewpoints we'll be considering in these pages, Christianity has perhaps least in common with the views of secular humanism—which is ironic, since humanism emerged in the soil of the West where Christianity has its deepest and most ancient roots. Indeed, it can be argued that secular humanism came into existence and has taken hold, to some degree at least, as a reaction to the confusion, oppression, and corruption that have dominated at times in the Christian world itself.

During the Middle Ages, when the church became an overwhelming power in the secular world, exercising its influence to create laws that suppressed individual liberties and coerced religious orthodoxy, it created animosities and stirred resentments that linger into our own day. Many of the American colonies were established by people fleeing this type of religious oppression. It should not be surprising, then, that the thought leaders who emerged from this milieu would exclude a religious perspective from their systems.

Still, the fact that religious leaders during a particular period of history misused their opportunities doesn't deny the relevance of the gospel. While we may abhor the unpleasant historical factors which influenced the rise of humanism and secularity, and admit the church's role in them, this does not mean that we have to buy into that system—however popular or authoritative it may seem. The apostle Paul wrote: "See to it that no one takes you captive through hollow and deceptive philosophy, which depends on human tradition and the basic principles of this world rather than on Christ." Colossians 2:8, NIV.

"Hollow and deceptive philosophy." "Human tradition." "The basic principles of this world." What better language could be used to describe secular humanism? It almost seems as if the apostle was able to look forward to our day and pinpoint the specific perspectives which offer the greatest threat to the gospel in the modern age!

But what can the Christian say to the secularist? How do we respond to his assertions? The arguments of the secularist do not seem hollow and deceptive to him. He doesn't feel confused. He thinks *we're* the ones who are clinging to traditions in the face of scientific evidence that debunks our belief system. So how should we react to this challenge?

Reaction 1: Acknowledge the good in secularism, but refuse to be intimidated by its assertion that it offers absolute, objective truth—particularly on issues outside its expertise.

There is a wide gap between the achievements of technology and the claims of its secularist philosophy. All that passes under the name of "science" isn't necessarily "scientific." Much of it is philosophical speculation done by scientists, and we must draw the line between the two.

Carl F. H. Henry, well-know Evangelical writer and editor, wrote in his book *Christian Countermoves in a Decadent Culture,* "Science has indeed expanded human convenience and comfort. But it has not made man wiser, better, or happier. The empirical method of knowing cannot illumine the supernatural world, cope with the moral realities of good and evil, or contend with the dilemmas of death and destiny. Science cannot even foresee the devastating ramifications of its own scientific achievements."

As long as we're able to distinguish between the technological expertise secularism offers and the philosophical extensions some scientists make—assertions that go far beyond the known into the realm of speculation—we'll have no difficulty relating to secularism. Albert Einstein was a remarkable scientist. But when he wrote in his book *What I Believe,* "To ponder interminably over the reason for one's own existence or the meaning of life in general seems to me, from an objective point of view, to be sheer folly," he was writing not as a scientist, but as an armchair philosopher—and his views carry no more authority than the next person's.

Reaction 2: Calmly assert your confidence in the viability of a world view based on the Scriptures and centered in the gospel.

It's very important to keep in mind that a person's presuppositions about the structure of life condition all that he does or says. There is no way to *know,* in an absolute, objective sense, anything about the meaning of life and death or the true order of existence. The answers we give to these fundamental questions are matters of faith, not certainty. We can *believe* them, but we can't *know* them.

The Christian world view is based on God's revelation in the Bible and on our sense of the "rightness" of that revelation. We cannot prove it. It cannot be subjected to the scientific method. Similarly, however, it cannot be disproved. It must be accepted or rejected on the basis of our response to the message itself.

Secularism claims to be scientific and would have us believe that the world view it proposes has the authority of objective analysis. This, however, is a myth. No one was there when the world was formed but God. No one had a hand in the formation of man but God. The prevailing views in the scientific community about how all things came to be are complex belief systems based on certain fragile presuppositions that are no more "provable" than the suppositions on which the religious person builds.

Take, for example, the fundamental cosmological theory on the "big bang." Scientists assert that all matter in the universe emerged from a tiny microdot of incredible, unimaginable power, which exploded the universe into existence billions of years ago. Everything in the universe is supposed to have come from that concentrated dot, too small for the naked eye to see. It's an interesting theory, and one that has been accepted by the majority of the scientific community. Yet a theory is all it is. Ask the scientist where this remarkable dot came from, and all he can do is shrug. There is no answer.

Or consider the odds against animate life emerging from lifeless matter in the earth's primordial state. The scientific fact is that there is no way to create life from nonlife. Yet science believes it *must* have happened and has gone on to build the incredibly complex edifice of evolution on the assumption that this impossible scenario somehow did happen.

In the face of this, is it so speculative to believe in a loving God who spoke the worlds into existence? The gospel message is the most liberating, challenging, and noble message the world has ever heard. It must stand or fall on the basis of its own inherent strength. And it is entirely *rational* for you to assert your confidence in it.

Reaction 3: Relate to the secularist as a person, distinct from secularism as a system, and offer him the same warmth and generosity of spirit you would like others to afford you.

The gospel is a message of hope. It speaks to the very real and legitimate human needs that every human being shares—and it does so in a way that secular humanism never can. When presented in its fulness, the gospel is able to instill faith and the noblest of aspirations in the human spirit. It can take a man from the humblest of beginnings and draw him to a stature unparalleled by what any other system could hope to do.

Rather than feeling *defensive* in the face of secularism's claims, we should be *bold* in forwarding the claims of the gospel—which are far more expansive than the claims of secularism. Where secularism offers only the limits of man's own capabilities, the gospel offers the vast resources of a loving God. Where secularism offers only a few short years of struggle, after which there is nothing, the gospel offers eternal life. Where secularism offers a view of human history with more of the same—more suffering, more inhumanity of man to man, more raping of our natural resources until the very world itself is decimated—the gospel offers the return of Jesus to usher in an age when all things will be new and better.

In our boldness at forwarding the gospel's claims, we should avoid acting out of religious bigotry, looking down our noses at someone merely because he doesn't see things just the way we do. It would be a horrible injustice for Christians to act in an un-Christian manner as they share the Christian message. Yet we all know it has happened—and far too often.

The appeal of the gospel lies in its inherent strength and beauty and in the transformation of character it can bring to the believer. We are false to the gospel when we attempt to coerce others into sharing our viewpoints or when we demean them for theirs. We must never forget that the most telling argument for the gospel is the charitable spirit of the individual Christian.

Against this, the cold, lifeless message of secularism has no defense.

Thought Questions:

1. In your response to the views of secular humanism, how do you deal with the idea of contingency—that is, everything that happens is caused by natural phenomena? Have you had personal experience with the supernatural?
2. Do you feel that there are moral absolutes today? What are they? The Ten Commandments? The golden rule? The love commandment?
3. Can you *prove* the truth of the Scriptures? Can the secularist *prove* the truth of evolution? How should the Christian relate to the diversity of ideas that flourish in our culture today?
4. How do you think Jesus would relate to a secular person? Would He argue with him? Would He burn his books? Would He turn his back on him?
5. In your estimation, what is the ultimate strength of the gospel?

Chapter 3

The Lure of the Gospel of Power

It is perhaps unfortunate that the secular person often first meets the claims of the gospel in the form of television preachers. While no one doubts that each of these individuals *means* well, it is often the case that the style and content of these media proclamations create as much confusion and offense to the secular person as they do encouragement and positive response. The pressure to draw larger and larger audiences, and to raise increasingly significant budgets, sometimes creates approaches that obscure the gospel itself.

In this chapter, we will consider one form of Christianity that certainly seems to have earned the descriptive term *exotic.* Please keep in mind as you read that the following comments in no way intentionally demean the sincerity of those considered. The criticisms stated relate only to the potential for confusing secular men and women on the fundamental issues of the gospel.

He struts across the stage, television cameras following his every move, capturing the intensity of his expression and the sheer electricity of his movements. He waves his Bible in the air to emphasize his point. He rolls quickly into the guttural sounds of an unknown tongue, speaking several sentences with eyes slightly glazed, and then slides back into regular speech with ease.

He leaps to the floor of the auditorium and runs along a row of supplicants, slapping each of them on the forehead, knocking them into the waiting arms of strategically placed aides. Row after row of the blind, the lame, and the halt follow, rushing to form a new line before he can get to them. Now he is using both hands, literally dancing down the line, slapping heads with a staccato rhythm. Shouts of "hallelujah!" and "praise God!" fill the room. Sweat pours down the evangelist's chiseled face, but still he continues until his strength is gone.

At last he slows, stumbles momentarily, and then pauses to catch his breath. He holds his hands up, signaling an end to the healing, and then slowly mounts the stage again. It's time to ask the television audience to send money.

Gospel Superstars on Stage

Television has given birth to a new age of media evangelists whose style and message, while drawing strength and historical roots from Pentecostalism, is distinctive and unusually potent. Some of the more prominent names include Kenneth Copeland, Jimmy Swaggart, Pat Robertson, Oral Roberts and his son Richard. And of course there's Jimmy Bakker, whose fall from grace threw TV evangelism into a panic and whose PTL show was taken over by Jerry Falwell. But these are only the glittering edge of a movement that is becoming the most powerful force in Christianity today.

All across America these charismatic evangelists weave their spell over the masses. Through a combination of slick production and sophisticated marketing, they present their messages in a package that is nearly irresistible. Their opinions are forthright and emphatic, and their message of instant health, gratuitous wealth, and Holy Ghost power is compelling. There is *authority* in their tone and *fire* in their eyes. They preach a gospel that emphasizes what God can do for the believer *now.* And it's a message that fills auditoriums across the nation and draws millions to their television sets week after week.

These evangelists of the media age are preaching the *gospel of power.* Unlike many of their more staid counterparts in the mainline Christian churches, these men (and a few women) pack an exotic impact that has brought hope and religious excitement to a mass audience that went largely untouched before them.

There is a pragmatic logic behind what the power gospelers are proposing. It reads: "Religion, if it's to be worth anything, ought to *do* something in your life. It should heal you when you're sick, bring you money when you're broke, and give you power over the devil—whether he manifests himself through classical demon possession or through enslavement to drugs, illicit sex, or alcohol." And like all forms of folk logic, this message makes a world of sense to those who respond. It's like Ben Franklin's "The Lord helps those who help themselves" or Abe Lincoln's "You can fool some of the people some of the time. . . ." Who could disagree? It's *obviously* true!

Yet *is* it?

The Gospel of Power and the Gospel of Grace

While there are some cautions relating to those preaching the gospel of power which demand expression—and this section of the book has been developed to do so—keep in mind that I'm not *against* them. I do feel that they are jogging down a theological fast track, preaching a media-driven message with some inherent difficulties. Yet they are, almost without exception, admirable, winsome people. Along with their unique emphasis, they are also preaching about the great themes of the Bible and proclaiming Jesus as the salvation for human need—which is certainly positive. And they are considerably more entertaining than the occasional preacher from the more mainline denominations who tries his hand at television preaching or the fundamentalist pew-pounders who seem so wholly preoccupied with the declining level of viewer donations.

The issue is whether or not the dominant message they are preaching—the gospel of power—for all its evident appeal, is cut precisely from the same cloth as the message Jesus brought—the gospel of grace.

The concept of various "gospels" isn't new. The apostle Paul saw them cropping up just a few years after the crucifixion of Jesus. He wrote to the Galatian believers, "I am astonished that you are so quickly deserting the one who called you by the grace of Christ and are turning to a different gospel—which is really no gospel at all." Galatians 1:6, 7, NIV. In a similar letter he chastised the Corinthian believers for turning away from the gospel and told them how foolish they were to accept those who preach "a Jesus other than the Jesus we preached . . . or a different gospel from the one you accepted." 2 Corinthians 11:4, NIV.

The true gospel, as Paul defined it, focused on "the grace of Christ," while the other "gospel," in each case, focused on man's efforts and claimed to provide the believer with tangible certainty about his spiritual authority. In the case of the Galatians, that certainty was found in obeying the law. In Corinth, it centered in exotic spiritual manifestations such as speaking in tongues and miraculous healing. Each of these situations is parallel to what happened with the children of Israel when they came out of slavery in Egypt. Moses introduced them to the invisible God who must be accepted by faith, but the people wanted a tangible god they could look at and feel. So they coerced Aaron, Moses' brother, into building them a god made out of gold.

It has never been easy for us humans to believe the gospel of grace. Human nature being what it is, we're always trying to create substitutes which are more tangible, more in keeping with the aspirations of the human spirit. We want to *do* something that will win God's favor and demonstrate our worth. We want a gospel that allows room for human contributions. We want to *see* something that confirms our beliefs. We aren't confortable with an invisible God who tells us to live by faith. We want all the buzzers and whistles. We want our religion *palpable.*

Which is why the gospel of power is so appealing. It brings the "pie in the sky by and by" right here into our hands, so that faith in unnecessary.

Of course, the gospel of power is not very new. Jesus, Himself encountered it. "The devil led him up to a high place and showed him in an instant all the kingdoms of the world. And he said to him, 'I will give you all their authority and splendor, for it has been given to me, and I can give it to anyone I want to. So if you worship me, it will all be yours.' Jesus answered, 'It is written: "Worship the Lord your God and serve him only."'" Luke 4:5-8, NIV.

Jesus wasn't tempted to sin with the power the devil offered, but the temptation was very real just the same. He was tempted to do good—at his pace, rather than God's. When He rejected the devil's offer, He wasn't rejecting rulership of the world. That had been promised Him. He rejected taking *then* what God had promised *later*—after the road to Calvary.

And that issue lies at the core of the difficulty posed by the gospel of power. It involves the temptation to have or do or display some very good, very "spiritual" things—but at *our* pace and in *our* way, rather than God's.

The gospel of power asks: Is it God's will that we should all be drab, passive, retiring men and women, unwilling to advance our ideas to take a vigorous position on any issue? Should we sit around in the lotus position each day, waiting for God to take care of all our problems, suffering silently and taking it on the chin?

And it answers: No! A million times No! There is power available by which we can take control of our lives. We Christians don't have to have sand kicked in our faces. We can go to battle with every expectation of winning. We can cast out devils; we can walk through fire; we can expect to be healthy, wealthy, and wise—here and now, rather than in the hereafter. The problems we face are evidences of our lack of faith. God surely doesn't want us to suffer. The power for victory is there if we'll just *claim* it!"

Clearly, one major appeal of the gospel of power is that it is so upbeat. It is positive. It is a gospel for winners. And who could be against winning?

No one. But remember, it was Vince Lombardi, *not God,* who said, "Winning isn't everything; it's the *only* thing." In God's economy, *how you play the game* is every bit as important.

The gospel of power is intriguing precisely because it speaks to something very basic in the human personality. But not all aspects of our personality are the most noble. That's why there are some gaping chuckholes in the theological fast track.

Chuckhole 1: In its emphasis on the need for constant miracles in the life of the believer, the gospel of power shows itself to be an impatient gospel.

The gospel of power says, "I want it all, and I want it now!" The path of suffering and character-building is wholly rejected in favor of the quick-fix, the shortcut to success—physically, financially and spiritually.

When the disciples saw the man blind from birth, as the story is recorded in John 9, they came to Jesus and said, "Rabbi, who sinned, this man or his parents, that he was born blind?" Verse 2, NIV. Attracted by the seductive appeal of the gospel of power, even in their day, the disciples were certain the tragedy was somebody's fault—and that if people just had enough faith, they'd never be sick or handicapped. Jesus answered them by saying, "Neither this man nor his parents sinned, . . . but this happened so that the work of God might be displayed in his life." Verse 3, NIV.

God had a purpose behind all those years of suffering. Now, many years later, that purpose was about to be revealed. Was the waiting pleasant? No. Was it essential? Absolutely. The waiting had a beneficial long-term effect on the blind man, who went on to become an eager disciple. His testimony went to the highest levels of Jewish government and became part of the biblical record to benefit all succeeding generations.

Sometimes, contrary to the quick-fix dictates of the gospel of power, our tragedy is allowed by a loving God because it helps us grow—or *could* if we responded to it patiently. "The wound which is borne in God's way brings a change of heart too salutary to regret," the Bible says, "but the hurt which is borne in the world's way brings death." 2 Corinthians 7:10, NEB.

Chuckhole 2: In its almost total focus on what God can do for the believer now, the gospel of power shows itself to be a materialistic gospel.

The gospel of power is a "what's in it for me?" approach to spiritual life. In this, it is very much an Americanized gospel. It is a natural extension of our bold, agressive Western style—which we display all over the world through economic clout, social impact, and political/military muscle. Our way of life is dedicated to getting *more* of whatever there is to get: more money, bigger cars, classier women (or men), and a bigger cut of the pie.

Those advocating the gospel of power couch even the specifically spiritual aspects of their message in terms of the dramatic and the exotic. They focus on healings, speaking in unknown tongues, casting out devils, and prophesying. They have little interest in the gentler, more subtle spiritual characteristics of the gospel, such as kindness, generosity, and faith.

When the apostle Paul wrote to the Corinthian church, where the gospel of power was running rampant, his message was one of restraint. It culminated in an appeal that the believers turn from their hunger for bigger and more dramatic spiritual experiences to emphasize "a better way," the way of love. See 1 Corinthians 12 and 13. Jesus' emphasis, in the way He lived and died, as well as in the words He spoke all during His ministry, was on *giving* rather than *getting,* on *serving* rather than *being served.* "Whoever wants to become great among you must be your servant, and whoever wants to be first must be your slave—just as the Son of Man did not come to be served, but to serve, and to give his life as a ransom for many." Matthew 20:26-28, NIV. This is an emphasis that runs totally counter to the emphasis that we so often see in the gospel of power.

Chuckhole 3: In its demand to have it all now, rather than wait for God's good time, the gospel of power shows itself to be an adolescent gospel.

Contemporary America is obsessed with the youth culture. We are driven by adolescent fantasies. We all want faces and bodies that look like we're eighteen. We spend billions of dollars on cosmetics, plastic surgery, and exercise equipment. We dress in styles that are "youngish," regardless of how foolish they make us look. And we go to great lengths to stay in touch with "what's happening," because being old-fashioned is the equivalent, today, of simply being *wrong*—and ranks high on the modern list of sins.

While most of the major proponents of the gospel of power are not young themselves, what they propose is the stuff of adolescent fantasies. Adults know that we all have to take the good with the bad, and that we put off temporary pleasure to assure long-term success. Our parents built this great nation, whose benefits we enjoy so fully, on that ethic. But adolescents reject all that, demanding sexual satisfaction at thirteen, economic independence at fifteen, and credibility for their ideas *now,* rather than later, when they've "paid their dues."

Adolescence is a time when the emotions run wild, pumped up by overactive hormones. It's a time when a determined pursuit after the greatest "high" seems to be more important than making reasoned judgments about the future. *Feeling* holds the primacy, setting aside logic, responsibility, and commitment.

This same spirit dominates the gospel of power. The gospel of power is the gospel of good feelings as one minister said, the baptism of the Holy Spirit felt "like electricity running up and down my spine!"

There isn't anything wrong with an adolescent gospel, as long as it is experienced by adolescent Christians, going through the natural process of change and development that causes them eventually to mature beyond it under God's tutelage. The gospel needs to speak to all of us, right where we are, and our perceptions of it should evolve with us as we develop. But the proponents of the gospel of power are like Peter Pan: they want to remain little boys all their lives and are willing to fight to do so. They declare that their version of the gospel *is* mature Christianity, and they look down at all others as weak, frail imitations. After all, *they've* got the power!

A Serious Matter of Emphasis

Since those preaching the gospel of power are clearly advocating Christian values and biblical themes, it would be a serious mistake to suggest that they aren't Christians or that they are somehow dangerous to the gospel itself. Christianity isn't an exclusive club, accepting only those who look alike, dress alike, and sound alike. However, it would be an equally serious mistake to argue that the differences between the gospel of power and the gospel of grace are merely a matter of style. The issues are more complex than how colorful we like our religion.

Just as impatient, materialistic, adolescent *behavior* can get us into trouble in our day-to-day lives, sometimes creating serious situations that compromise our whole futures, so impatient, materialistic, adolescent *religion* can hinder—or even turn back—our spiritual growth and development.

Doesn't the Bible talk about Holy Ghost power? Of course it does. Doesn't it describe healings, speaking in tongues, and all the other components emphasized in the gospel of power? Certainly. It talks about walking through scorpions' nests without being stung, holding snakes without being bitten, and feeding 5,000 people from a few loaves of bread and a couple of fish. The miraculous and the spectacular certainly do form an important part of the Christian experience.

But when they become the *focus* rather than lying at the periphery, the *objective and passion* rather than an identifying sign, these emphases distract our attention from the eternal principles of God's grace. They hinder our appropriate response of faith, hope, and love, which lie at the core of the message of Jesus Christ.

When Jesus was brought before King Herod just prior to His crucifixion, it was in the king's power to release Him. All Herod demanded from Jesus was that He perform a miracle.

This was not the first time Jesus had faced this demand. With increasing frequency during His ministry, people came to Him for miracles. Toward the end, the population considered Him little more than an itinerant magician, there to entertain them and bring awe and wonder into their drab lives.

Jesus refused Herod's request, knowing full well that it would bring on the sufferings of the cross. Why? Because He wanted people to listen to the gospel of grace, not be drawn merely by the gospel of power. He knew that another miracle would save no one, but accepting the salvation provided by His death would save the world.

Ultimately, the danger of the gospel of power is that it distracts us from the gospel of grace. The lure of the spectacular blinds us to the appeal of the profound. The lofty way of the mountaintop takes away our stomach for the humbling way of the cross. The trumpets and cymbals so overwhelm us that we cannot hear the still, small voice of the Holy Spirit.

Robert Frost, in his poem, "The Road Not Taken," stated it well:

> "Two roads diverged in a wood, and I—
> I took the one less travelled by,
> And that has made all the difference."

The normal Christian life isn't all bells and whistles. Often it is the quiet time we spend one-on-one with our God. Learning to trust Him more. And listening as he works to develop our characters. Above all, the *focus* in the Christian life should be not on what *we* can do, but on what *God* has done, as revealed in the gospel of grace.

Thought Questions:

1. How do you feel about the assertion that if religion is worth anything, it ought to *do* something in your life? What would you expect it to do?
2. Do you feel that positioning the gospel of power against the gospel of grace is fair?
3. In your opinion, do poverty, illness, and other personal problems show that you lack faith? Does it automatically

follow that if we just ask God for riches, good health, and personal success, he will bring these to us? Does God ever say No or Wait?

4. What, in your opinion, is the relationship between miracles and faith? Does faith produce miracles? Can miracles ever inhibit faith?
5. Are all Christians the same? Are there varieties of Christian experience? How wide might these varieties be and still be within the framework of Christianity?

Chapter 4:
The Looming Specter of the Christian Radical Right

"God said it. I believe it. That settles it. And, brother, *you* better believe it, too!"

Christianity with a chip on its shoulder. The church turned into a "lean, mean fighting machine." Bully-boy religion with a clinched fist, drawing a line in the sand and daring anyone to cross it. One of the more frightening specters on the horizon today is the emergence of a politically potent, angry, and mean-spirited Christian radical right.

What is the Christian radical right?

Out at the periphery of the Christian fellowship is a growing group of believers who see themselves as "saviors" of the Christian world. They are right-wing extremists who are committed to dramatic changes in our culture that would result in an Old Testament type theocracy. This New Religious Right would turn America into a "Christian nation," modeled according to their own vision, without any vestiges of the pluralism we see today. Faith in God would be mandated. Religious orthodoxy would be required. A state religion would control the lives of every man, woman and child in our nation—resolving the many problems we face today by the iron fist of religious law. Crimes against God's law, such as homosexuality, Sabbath breaking, apostasy, and incorrigibility in children, would receive the death penalty.

In the February 20, 1987 issue of *Christianity Today*, author Rodney Clapp's article, "Democracy as Heresy," provides an in depth analysis of the New Religious Right. He points out that key proponents of what has been called Christian Reconstructionism, R. J. Rushdoony, Gary North, and Greg Bahnsen, envision a society where "every single stroke of the law must be seen by the Christian as applicable to this very age between the advents of Christ."

In his book, *Religion in the Secular City: Toward a Postmodern Theology*, theologian Harvey Cox writes, "Mass media fundamentalism . . . presents a theology that celebrates patriotism, individual success, and a political spectrum ranging from the moderately conservative to the far, far right."

It's this fringe at the "far, far right" that offers unique challenges to the gospel.

Of all the groups we'll consider in these pages, the Christian radical right is in many ways the most difficult challenge. Their theology isn't that diverse from the mainstream of Christianity, though it is sometimes carried to extremes—as in the case of their belief that Christ's kingdom will be set up wholesale on Earth before He returns. The things they stand for are generally good: patriotism, motherhood, and confidence in the Bible. T.V. evangelists Pat Robertson and James Kennedy have often had Reconstructionists on their programs, but refuse to endorse their beliefs in entirety. In short, the New Religious Right represents ideas that sound familiar and make sense to an increasing number of Christians.

But the *way* they go about supporting these causes, and the end result they envision, is in some ways a greater departure from the spirit of Jesus Christ than is the case with any of the other groups we're discussing in his book. And in a sense they pose the greatest threat—because not only do they diverge widely from the spirit of the gospel, but their own harsh spirit serves to turn vast numbers of unchurched people away from the Christian faith.

The Roots of Reactionary Christianity

Interestingly enough, the Christian radical right seems to have taken its marching orders from the very liberals it detests so utterly. During the 60s and 70s, liberal politicians and political activists were able to push into law sweeping programs that aided the disadvantaged and disenfranchised of our society. The Civil Rights Act of 1964 is only the most well-publicized of these many changes in our national way of life—changes which transpired, to some degree at least, because thousands of black Americans and college-age students of all races took to the streets and marched through our nation's cities in great orchestrated campaigns to show their strength and unity.

The message the radical right received from all this was that if you want something done in America, get organized as a political force. Emulating Black Power, they created their own version of White Power, using many of the same strategies and techniques. The "old-fashioned" ideas of the separation of church and state, which were so thoroughly embraced by our nation's founding fathers, were suddenly tossed aside. If the state wasn't willing to be supportive to rightist causes, then the state needed overhauling. The idea of creating a *theocracy*, a church-run state, caught hold. "Sending Washington a message" became a common theme from Christian radical rightist pulpits and television platforms across America.

It took a few years for reactionary Christianity to get itself organized, but in the national elections of 1976, 1980, and 1984, it emerged as one of the most dominant forces in American politics. Preachers were no longer passive voices for the status-quo, urging their parishioners to acts of love and understanding. Sermons about "turning the other cheek" were tossed in the trash compactor, to be replaced by new sermons on political activism, and pleas for greater and greater financial contributions to support the aggressive campaign that needed to be run. Preachers now became strident voices denouncing the policies of the government, with blocks of votes to wave under the noses of those willing to come out in favor of right-wing issues.

The Christian radical right had arrived—and it was prepared to fight.

Putting the Christian Radical Right in Perspective

In a manner similar to the other "exotic" belief-systems we're examining within the Christian community, the Christian radical right displays tendencies that can easily distract from the gospel. Worse, it represents a world view that poses some very alarming dangers to the body of Christ. The following observations are not designed to condemn the Christian radical right. Rather, they are intended to serve as a caution relative to some of its more extreme aspects.

Observation 1: One of the difficulties in knowing just how to deal with the Christian radical right is that it frequently masquerades as Christian conservatism or fundamentalism.

Mainstream Christianity is a wide circle, encompassing various perspectives and emphases. Just as those promoting the gospel of power are an extreme version of those who very legitimately emphasize enthusiasm and exuberance in their faith and worship, and who believe, correctly, that we can expect God to *act* in our lives, the Christian radical right is an extreme element extending in a bizarre fashion from Christian conservatism.

Conservative and fundamentalist believers have always played a key role in maintaining balance within the broad Christian fellowship, offering a very important point of view in the wide spectrum of Christian beliefs. It is almost a truism that we tend to get more conservative as we grow older. And it may well be that such a pattern is essential for the health of the church. We need those with the courage to venture out into new thinking, and we need those who can give the sage counsel of the traditions which have stood the test of time. The church has been enriched by the presence of both.

By nature, conservatism infers a quiet confidence in the virtues which have stood the test of time. Conservative people dress demurely, they don't make fools of themselves at parties, and they speak softly. We expect our parents to be conservative—always there when we need them, and firm as a rock in their love. We expect bankers and funeral directors to be conservative. Walter Cronkite and Mr. Roger's Neighborhood are forces for conservatism.

But the Christian radical right is anything but conservative in its demeanor and approach to life. Its adherents are loud, aggressive, and insistent on change. They pound pulpits and intimidate people. They threaten dire consequences for those who dare to cross them. And when they smile, there is *steel* in their eyes.

Roland Hegsted, editor of *Liberty* magazine, has insightfully observed that the problem we face with the Christian radical right is not that they are bad people trying to make others bad, but that they are good people, trying to *make* others good—and willing to go to whatever lengths are necessary to impose that goodness.

It does both the conservative and fundamentalist traditions in the church a disservice to confuse them with the Christian radical right.

Observation 2: The Christian radical right allows no room in its definition of true Christianity for those who diverge at all from its view.

While this book is an effort to take a careful look at some of the "exotic beliefs" current in and outside the church, it is, hopefully, a generous review. As Christians, we need to show acceptance of those who see things differently from us, even when they're on the very periphery of the Christian family, or when we disagree thoroughly with some of their views.

Unfortunately, the Christian radical right does not share this commitment.

There is no room for pluralism within the New Religious Right. You're either on the right side, or you're history—or would be, if they could achieve sufficient power to make their preferences stick.

It should be a matter of concern to all Christians just what might happen in this country if the Christian radical right were able to achieve the political power they presently seek so diligently. Where might the lines be drawn on what is and isn't an acceptable expression of Christian faith? And what measures might be put in place to assure the demanded level of conformity to the theological and behavioral beliefs of those in power? In their planned society, those whose beliefs don't quite match up with Reconstructionist views will be classed with atheists, perverts, and criminals—and all aimed toward the gallows. They even recommend a return to slavery as a means for eliminating the welfare state!

The idea that Christians should take an active role in the political structure of the nations where they live has received considerable debate over the years. Our nation's founding fathers were concerned over this issue, and went to some lengths to make separation of church and state a fundamental part of our nation's creed.

It seems a better and better idea these days.

A pluralistic society, such as we have today, is far from perfect. There are some very real and continuing problems that demand our attention. But a pluralistic society allows us the freedom to be who we are, rather than who someone else wants us to be, and it frees us to share the gospel according to our individual consciences. Every society this side of heaven will have problems, but the freedoms we enjoy in America today are a very precious heritage we dare not allow anyone to take away—even for the most religious of motives.

Observation 3: The Christian radical right represents a dangerous over-reaction to the mere presence of alternative world views in the idea marketplace.

Do you remember, when you were a child, how all the comic books had advertisements for Charles Atlas body-building equipment? (Or am I dating myself?) One story line had a skinny boy lying in the sand at the beach with his girlfriend, when this big bruiser comes by and kicks sand in his face. While he sits there helpless, his girl walks off with Mr. Muscle. The boy determines to do something about this, so he orders the Charles Atlas program and a few weeks later comes back to the beach and beats up on the guy who stole his girl.

This is the fantasy of the Christian radical right. The combined forces of secularism, communism, liberalism, intellectualism—and all the other "isms" in the world today—have come along and kicked sand in the faces of reactionary Christians. And they are about to get even.

Reactionary Christianity is like the skinny kid in its insecurity. It is desperate for some way to build itself up, so that the big guys on the street of ideas won't pick on it. The *Christianity Today* article cited earlier refers to Gary North's belief that, "the instructions of the Sermon on the Mount were intended for a 'captive' people, and that when Christians come to dominate a culture they no longer need turn the other cheek to the aggressor but may 'bust him in the chops.' "

This is a tragic attitude to see in a Christian. *God* isn't intimidated by anyone. His truth doesn't require our arrogance to substantiate it. And we don't need to over-react to the errors around us in order to stand for truth. *If we don't have faith that God's truth will prevail, we're on the wrong side.*

The danger in all this is that we'll get so caught up in what we're *against*, that we'll lose sight of what we're *for*. During the explosive early years of the Christian church, Christians weren't in the majority. They were often persecuted and ridiculed. Yet the church thrived. The fact that believers did not have a "Christian nation" in which to witness was no hindrance to the progress of the gospel. It was only when the church became large and powerful that ugly things began happening in the name of Christ.

There is a message here we dare not ignore.

Observation 4: In its preoccupation with doing God's work for Him, the Christian radical right shows a distressing spiritual arrogance.

In their concern to defend God against all comers, reactionary Christians are denying the power of God to take care of Himself. It's so easy for us to fall into the trap of believing that God is depending on *us* to do His work for Him—as though He is incapable of achieving His own ends without our direction.

This is, at root, a form of spiritual arrogance. And this arrogance, in its many manifestations, is one of the least attractive characteristics of the Christian radical right.

God does use us to further His work in the world. The witness of faith is one of the most powerful tools He has to win men and women to Himself. We *are* important in God's plans. But there is a world of difference between *being used* and *being the user*. Reactionary Christians have taken the sword out of God's hands and are wielding it themselves. They have established the spiritual agenda, and are promoting it with the greatest enthusiasm.

If God is God, He is able to raise up the very stones in the ground to proclaim His message. We are *privileged* to work with Him; we're not doing Him a *favor*.

Humility—especially spiritual humility—is good for the soul. And in this regard, the Christian radical right needs a soul transplant.

Observation 5: The Christian radical right, in its gospel of confrontation, is out of harmony with the spirit of Jesus Christ.

Jesus brought to this planet a message of love. He told of a loving father who longed for the return of his prodigal son—and never stopped loving him, even when the son had fallen into the grip of sin. He told of a shepherd who left the warmth and safety of the sheepfold to go out into the elements in search of his one lost sheep. He told of a city set on a hill, with a light that shines through the dark night as a beacon for all who will be drawn.

But reactionary Christianity has lost sight of the message of Jesus, and has substituted in its place a message of confrontation and resentment. Too preoccupied with gaining the victory, and too unconcerned with how it is to be achieved, it misses the whole point. Reactionary Christianity knows all the words in the gospel song, but has completely forgotten the melody.

Judas Iscariot is in some ways a good illustration of this approach. He was in a sense the most committed of Jesus' disciples. No one could have been more enthusiastic for the social changes the message of Jesus suggested. Judas' problem was that he was committed, but not to the gospel. He wanted so much for the kingdom of God to be established that he went to the extreme of trying to force Jesus' hand—believing he knew better than God how the kingdom should be inaugurated. He hanged himself when things didn't work out the way he expected.

The message Jesus brought is of a God who loves His children too much to let them go, who sent His own Son to die in mankind's place so that the world might be saved. It is a message of compassion and generosity, a message imbued with such forgiveness that it almost boggles the mind.

The Christian radical right has no time for such foolishness. It has a world to conquer.

Living the Life of Faith

While we have never received directive from God that we should allow the bullies in life to kick sand in our faces, neither do we have one to *be* such bullies ourselves. The life of faith is not a passive life. In accepting Jesus, we aren't giving up our ability for doing battle with evil. But the apostle Paul speaks about spiritual warfare fought with a different set of weapons from those used by the adversary. He counsels us, "*Then put on the garments that suit God's chosen people, his own, his beloved: compassion, kindness, humility, gentleness, patience.* Be forbearing with one another, and forgiving, where any of you has cause for complaint: you must forgive as the Lord forgave you. To crown all, there must be love, to bind all together and complete the whole. Let Christ's peace be arbiter in your hearts; to this peace you were called as members of a single body. And be filled with gratitude. Let the message of

Christ dwell among you in all its richness." Colossians 3:12-16, NEB.

This portrait of the Christian fits well with a world view that sees God in control of history, moving events along at His own pace, according to His schedule. The Christian radical right would do well to study it a little more closely. God *is* God. His plans *will* prevail. Our usefulness to Him has more to do with providing a lost and confused world with a witness of compassion, kindness, humility, gentleness and patience than with achieving and wielding political power.

Chapter 5
The Curious World of the Christian Cults

We move now to viewpoints considerably more distant from traditional Christianity. It is not our purpose to assert that those in the Christian cults are *not* true Christians. Instead, our intent is to observe those elements in their belief systems which pose difficulties to a clear perception of the gospel—and for that reason need to be clearly identified for what they are. While the word *heresy* may seem a little harsh in our pluralistic age, we need to recognize that the belief systems within the Christian cults often diverge from biblical truth in basic and significant ways. As individual Christians, it makes good sense that we have some fairly ordered plans for how we will deal with the challenge they offer.

The rising interest in religion noted by recent national surveys is not reflected in church attendance patterns in mainline Christian churches. Instead, much of this renewed interest has found a home in Neo-Pentecostalism and in the various Christian sects and cults. People want to touch something powerful. They're interested in religious systems which promise something unique, either in terms of spiritual power or point of view.

This, the Christian cults offer in full supply.

Who *are* the Christian cultists? Of the various groups that have sprung into existence during the past century or two, most have gradually evolved into reasonably mainstream denominations, with only a few rather innocuous differences of belief or practice to separate them from the more traditional denominations. Those slightly further from the center we sometimes refer to as *sects.* Those still further afield we usually call *cults*. Sects are a little different from denominations, having drifted slightly from mainstream, but are still generally viewed as OK. Even Neo-Pentecostalism, or the charismatic movement, as it's sometimes called, has settled into spiritual respectability. Television evangelist Pat Robertson occupies such a centrist position that he's been accounted a serious candidate for the Presidency.

Cults, on the other hand, are considered very questionable, perhaps even bad or dangerous. A few groups, such as the Jehovah's Witnesses, the Mormons, and the Christian Scientists—to note only some of the larger, more visible representatives of the Christian cults—have developed theologies which diverge so widely from mainstream Christianity that it is difficult to imagine their being readily integrated back into the general flow. The territory they've staked out, involving their beliefs about God, man, and the thrust of human history, is too exotic to merge comfortably with the broad teachings of Scripture.

What Makes a Cult a Cult?

The word *cult* is not, in its root meaning, a pejorative term. It comes from the same root as the word *cultivate.* It means "the springing up or emergence of a system of beliefs or a group of believers." However, in today's usage, it is generally felt to be a religious "bad word." We generally don't use it to describe anyone we like. Indeed, it is frequently used with judgmental overtones, inferring a certain amount of strangeness—perhaps even a touch of the bizarre.

Most people don't like their group to be called a cult, and their members don't take kindly to being called cultists. Would you? Or I?

An argument could be made for rejecting the use of the word *cult* entirely. If we're employing it as a form of "baptized" name-calling, then it is hardly a noble thing to do. It merely irritates those so named. But since the nomenclature has been used for quite some time in a reasonably scholarly, nonaccusatory setting, as a term to identify those groups whose uniqueness sets them quite outside the circle of orthodoxy, we'll continue to use it here—but with advisement.

Many cults, of course, involve no connection with Christianity at all. Cultic religious systems have existed down through the centuries, covering the full spectrum from the reasonably innocuous to the incredibly bizarre and horribly vicious. We would certainly name Satanism a cult, for example. Charles Manson and his followers formed a cult.

Those generally termed "Christian cultists," however, see themselves as being just as fully Christian as any other body of believers. They acknowledge that their belief systems diverge from the larger body of Christian beliefs in many significant ways, but they don't see that as a negative. Instead, they usually view themselves as missionaries to the church at large, commissioned to help the rest of the family "see the light"—meaning, of course, their unique version of the Christian faith.

Relating to the Christian Cultists

In relating to the Christian cultists, it's important to keep in mind that the largest number of their believers are extremely sincere and deeply committed. They are *good* people. The Jonestown fanaticism isn't characteristic of all Christian cultists. They usually aren't wild-eyed radicals, out to undermine the church and steal away our babies. Instead, Christian cultists are generally pretty much like the rest of us.

There are two kinds of cultists: First are those who were born into families that were members of churches with some rather exotic belief systems. They've grown up with these beliefs, which now seem quite *ordinary* to them. Second are those who were contacted by representatives of Christian cultic organizations at times when they were in deep spiritual need and have found in the churches they've joined the type of support they've needed. Generally, they consider any unconventional beliefs of their new religion to be an insignificant price to pay for the acceptance they now enjoy.

We're not going to spend a great deal of time, here, reciting or refuting the specific beliefs of the various Christian cults. There are several good books in print that do this with faithfulness and insight. If you're interested in knowing more about these beliefs in detail, I'd suggest you go to a Christian bookstore and pick up one of these books from what is usually quite an extensive section dedicated to the task of debunking the cults. Some of them are a little more strident in tone than others, but they're almost all reasonably informative.

As you've no doubt picked up by now, I strongly believe there is room in the Christian family for varying opinions on a broad spectrum of religious topics—even some that are fairly basic. However, it's important to avoid allowing this pluralistic generosity to cloud the fundamentals of the Christian faith. Following are a few cautions relative to the beliefs and practices of the Christian cultists.

Caution 1: In relating to the Christian cultists, don't accept any theological premise that shifts the gospel off center stage.

The uniqueness of the Christian message is not its ethical system, its supernatural manifestations, or its promise of spiritual power or eternal reward. Other systems offer similar religious elements. *What makes Christianity unique is the gospel: God doing for mankind what we couldn't do for ourselves. God sending His own Son as a sacrifice, substituting Himself for us, dying so that we might live.* And anyone who leads us to place our attention on anything but the sacrifice at Calvary—whatever that distraction may be—is, by definition, introducing cultic elements into his beliefs.

Legalism, for example, is by this definition a cultic teaching, even though it is quite common among all Christian groups. It puts human behavior at the center, displacing the gospel as our posture in approaching God. Similarly, Neo-Pentecostalism puts gifts of the Spirit on center stage.

Mormonism puts our quest for personal godhood there. And the Jehovah's Witnesses put the vindication of God's character at the center. Note that these are mostly very good things. What's wrong in each situation is that peripheral issues have been allowed to occupy the attention, getting in the way of a clear perception of the gospel.

Cultic attitudes or behavior are often quite evident in groups we would not normally identify as cults. Roman Catholicism, for example, representing by far the largest segment of the Christian community, and serving as the arena where most of the theological debates have been fought down through the centuries, has been guilty at times of allowing its focus to shift significantly from the gospel with tragic result. The Protestant Reformation, which splintered the church into many denominations, didn't really take place over matters of theology, *per se.* There were theologians within the Roman Catholic Church then who believed as fervently in righteousness by faith as did the Reformers. The Reformation really took place because the Roman Catholic Church elected to take a cultic posture on the issue of *authority.* Roman Catholic leaders became so preoccupied with their right to determine orthodoxy that men like Martin Luther and John Calvin had no choice but to strike out on their own.

The gospel is our great treasure. It's what separates Christianity from Buddhism, Hinduism, Shintoism, Communism, Secularism, and all the other "isms" in the world. We must reject all efforts to displace it with human inventions, however spiritual, authoritative, or spectacular they may seem.

Caution 2: Avoid the losing proposition of trying to argue the Bible with a Christian cultist.

Don't misunderstand me. There is no reason to fear an honest discussion of biblical truth with any person at any time. The gospel is well able to stand on its own in any discussion.

But what happens when you sit down to do a Bible study with a Christian cultist is *not* a discussion. The word *discussion* assumes two reasonably intelligent and informed people sitting down to consider the merits of varying viewpoints—including some give-and-take based on a fair review of each perspective. This doesn't happen during Bible study with a cultist.

The problem is that while members of the Christian cults are very knowledgeable about their own belief systems, *they are generally wholly ignorant of the broad teachings of Scripture and fundamentally uninterested in learning.* They are there not to *discuss* but to *indoctrinate.* All they know is the verses of Scripture that fit the message they've come to present and strategies they've been taught as methods for achieving this indoctrination.

I'm not asserting this in any way to demean the preparation given the Christian cultist. His training is extremely good at doing what it was designed to do. It's a very effective way of preparing a group of people for debate—as long as *they* remain in control of the subject matter. If you've ever sat down to study the Bible with one of their representatives, you know how powerful a tool this training is.

But it is wholly at odds with true Bible study.

Ask a member of a Christian cult to do some exegesis on a passage of Scripture not directly tied into his planned presentation, and all you'll draw is a dull stare. He'll tell you he hasn't studied that part of Scripture yet or that he'll need to bring with him the next time someone who can answer your question better than he can. But when that other person arrives, you'll find yourself drawn away from the issue you wanted to discuss back into the familiar ground of the group's theological interest.

Trying to argue the Bible with Christian cultists is a no-win situation. They don't understand the broad sweep of Christian teachings that has been hammered out over centuries of careful study and honest debate. All they know is the narrow field of focus they've been taught. Other than the texts they've memorized—which can involve a large, complex system of connected verses—the Bible is unfamiliar ground to them, about which they're virtually as unsophisticated as the totally unchurched secularist.

There's no reason to be rude to the Christian cultist who wants to argue the Bible with you (termed "study the Bible with you"). You don't need to slam the door in his or her face or say nasty things. Simply refuse the offer with graciousness and kindness. Observe firmly that he or she has nothing to offer that would interest you.

Caution 3: Reject the intimidation that comes from confusing the Christian cultist's religious fervor with spirituality.

Christian cultists often put the rest of us to shame by the fervor with which they pursue their beliefs. They commit vast amounts of time, energy, and money to the cause, usually averaging far more of each than would be the case with the typical Christian. Seeing this, many of us are tempted to feel guilty over our commitment and wonder, perhaps, if the spirituality of these people surpasses ours. Some might even wonder whether all that commitment might not signal a more potent belief system than ours.

Don't believe it.

There are two aspects to this issue: (1) we often *should* do far more than we do, and deserve to feel a little ashamed of ourselves; and (2) we need to keep in mind that the Christian cultist does what he does for reasons that often don't coincide at all with the gospel. The challenge to do more of the good things we ought to do as children of God will always be with us. But if we're trying to work our way to heaven by our good deeds—which is what the Christian cultist is often attempting to do—we're *denying* the gospel.

True spiritual enthusiasm springs up in the heart of the person who rejoices over what God has done for him. It is love in action, leading him into self-sacrifice and a broad scope of actions he might not otherwise perform. At the extreme end of the spectrum, it leads even to martyrdom.

But religious acts performed with an eye to the scoreboard are repugnant to God.

Because it's impossible for any of us to read another

person's heart, there's no way we can test motivation. We can't look at another person's behavior and tell *why* he's doing what he's doing. Neither should we try. When we see someone from one of the Christian cults following his round of activities, there is no need for us to think, "Well, he's only doing it to buy his way into heaven." That's not the point. What we need to do is search our own hearts to discover how sincerely we're seeking God's presence in our lives—because we'll never become more committed to God merely by trying to "pump up" commitment in emulation of what we see in another.

Keep clearly in mind this one principle: *Commitment is a byproduct of relationship. We become more committed by spending time "beholding Jesus" in the Scriptures, appreciating more and more fully all that God has done for us.* There aren't any shortcuts.

Caution 4: When reacting to the aggressiveness of the Christian cultist, keep a balance between Christian courtesy and Christian firmness.

It's difficult, sometimes, to treat others with kindness, sympathy, and generosity when they're "in our faces" all the time. Christian cultists often seem so aggressive in their commitment to persuading us that we ought to see things their way that they drive us to the point of anger, creating in us a contentious spirit.

It is never right to be rude to people. When we find ourselves doing it, we should never deceive ourselves into thinking we are displaying the character of Jesus Christ. Rarely is indignation truly "righteous." We've usually just lost our temper. There is never a time when Christian courtesy can be abandoned in favor of a rough, petulant manner that merely reflects back what we're receiving.

On the other hand, neither are we required to endure the pressures some Christian cultists would put us under without giving *some* response.

This is where what I like to call "Christian firmness" comes into play. Christian firmness is a solid wall of spiritual confidence. It involves a joyous spirit and an unmoving certainty. We can smile at people, shake their hands with warmth, and tell them with all sincerity that we just don't have the time, interest, or inclination to listen to them. We respect them as brothers or sisters in Christ, we are impressed by their sincerity, and we have no ax to grind with their theology, but we're not available for the type of debate they'd like to entertain.

Try it. It's a powerful posture.

There has been a tendency for mainline Christians to discount the witness of the Christian cultists, relegating them to the dustbin of ideas. This is a dangerous attitude. While the idea systems of the cultists may seem strange to us, it's important to acknowledge their vigor and the attractiveness they hold for large numbers of people.

What makes these people and their teachings so attractive?

We've alluded to some reasons already, but we can summarize by admitting that for many people, the cult churches fill the same spiritual void that other, more mainstream churches have traditionally filled. People sense the spiritual, the mystical, the supernatural, in these contexts, just as they might in a Roman Catholic cathedral, a Pentecostal healing service, or a Baptist call down the sawdust trail.

Rather than building a wall to keep the Christian cultists out of our fellowship, we would be more in tune with the spirit of Christ to build bridges of love and acceptance to them. Keep in mind that every church was considered a cult in its infancy—including the early Christian church in the Roman Empire.

While the Christian cultists are on the periphery of biblical truth, they often share a commitment to many aspects of God's revelation. They are not our adversaries or enemies. Just as we accept into our physical families those who don't quite "fit in," we should be generous with those who are theologically a little odd. They're still family, and they need our love.

We just can't allow them to determine our theology.

Thought Questions:

1. Where would you draw the line between being pluralistic enough to be friendly toward those who diverge from fundamental biblical truth and being faithful to the gospel? Is it possible to be too accepting? Is it possible to be too spiritually arrogant?
2. Is it possible to be very sincere and very wrong at the same time? Does it matter what you believe, so long as you have faith?
3. What is it that makes the gospel different from all the various emphases within the Christian cults? How important is that difference?
4. Have you observed cultic behaviors and attitudes within *your* fellowship? Would you recognize them if they were there? List some examples.
5. Why is it fruitless to argue the Bible with a Christian cultist? What should you do instead?
6. Is there a difference between "fervor" and "faith"? What is the difference? Is one more important than the other?

Chapter 6

The Astrology Scam

As we observed in the last chapter, even the Christian cultists operate within a framework of close proximity to the gospel. At least we all speak the same language. Outside the circle of the Christian world view, however, are numerous belief systems that have little or nothing in common with the gospel. Some of them are more aggressive than others, offering a direct challenge to Christian concepts. A few are quite subtle, not directly competing in the idea marketplace, but merely slipping into some of the gaps.

One of these is astrology. Few Christians really take astrology seriously. It's classed with science fiction and fantasy, orbiting in our minds somewhere alongside stories about people who claim to have been taken for rides in flying saucers or seen the Loch Ness monster. We don't consider it a threat.

In the chapter that follows, I want to show that the impact of astrology is a little more complex than we might think. The issue is not so much whether a person glances at his or her horoscope each day. The issue is—well, you'll see.

"Hey, baby, what's your sign?"

The come-on is pure singles' jargon. Shallow and crude, perhaps, but everybody knows it for a casual opener. The questioner isn't interested in a discussion on astrology—he's just trying to hit on an attractive woman (or man).

You may not move in the singles' circuit, but you're likely to hear similar words just about anywhere these days. If you'll think about it, you'll probably agree that astrology is a pervasive factor in modern life. We use terms with astrological derivation every day. We talk about our "fate" or "lot in life." We joke about luck, or being born under a "lucky star." We comment about the "age" we're living in. But let's keep things in perspective: The millions of Americans who faithfully look up their horoscope in the newspaper each morning aren't believers in the ancient Persian religions from which the signs of the zodiac sprang. If you asked them if they *really* believe the stars control their destiny, most would grin and say, "Well, no, probably not—but it's remarkable how often my horoscope is accurate!"

There *are* serious devotees of astrology, of course—people who are deeply enmeshed in it as an occult theology. There are also those on the fringes of the occult world who make a living by creating horoscopes for magazines, newspapers, or individuals, including many of the very wealthy and famous. Most of these practitioners are charlatans, making a good living off the curiosity and gullibility of the public. They don't *believe* in what they're doing; they just believe in the money it makes them.

That so many have allowed themselves to be bilked in this manner is sad, but this is not where the real *astrology scam* is to be found. Charlatans and occultists pose dangers we all need to note and avoid, especially since it's so easy to slip into this world without even realizing it's happening. But the real danger from astrology is far more subtle and pervasive. It has to do with how astrology and other systems which share its major thrust—including some frequently expressed from Christian pulpits—impact on our behaviors and attitudes toward life. In the pages that follow I would like for you to consider with me several important points about astrology.

Consideration 1: Astrology's apparent successes are often simply the result of self-fulfilling prophecies.

Let's first consider astrology at its most pragmatic level: Does it *work?* While this is often the initial question people ask about astrology, at a very basic level it's the *wrong* question. It misses the key issue. Whether or not astrology works has little to do with its truth or falsehood as a system, because it can work for reasons that have nothing to do with its inherent nature. The tricks a magician does on stage *work,* but that doesn't mean he possesses magical powers. It just means he's good at his craft, causing the audience to focus on what he wants them to see, and *only* that. It has been humorously observed that salesmen, politicians, and tax accountants display similar skills.

Still, the question deserves an answer. *Does astrology work?*

Yes, it often does.

But a better question would be, *Why* does it work? Is it because the stars control our destiny? Is there some mystic power that pushes each of us toward a preordained pattern in life, over which we have no control? Are we victims of a fate that we cannot escape, regardless of what we believe or do?

The ancient astrologers put Earth at the center of the universe and segmented the heavens into twelve signs of the zodiac, an imaginary belt in the evening sky eighteen degrees wide that encompasses all the major planets except those they didn't know existed. They claimed the ability to predict the supposed influences of the stars on human affairs by their positions.

Astrology had all but died out until the mid-nineteenth century, when it was revived in Great Britain. It has now grown on both sides of the Atlantic until it once again rivals more traditional religions as a source from which countless of the faithful draw insight and guidance. Thousands wouldn't dream of beginning their day without checking to see what counsel their favorite horoscope source offers them.

When our horoscopes prove accurate, there *is* a power at work—a decided power, with profound and lasting impact. But it's the power of self-fulfilling prophecies, not the power of the stars.

An important psychological truth about human behavior is that life is generally pretty much what we expect it to be. If we believe certain things will happen to us, either in a positive or negative sense, those things have a way of happening. But they happen, not as a result of fate or some preconceived pattern into which we're tied; they happen because at a subconscious level we *aim* ourselves in those directions.

The impact of self-fulfilling prophesies can be very real and very damaging. If I think I'm going to be a loser in life's interactions, the chances are very good I will be, simply because my attitude predisposes me to failure. Have you ever noticed how a dog tends to attack if it senses that a person is afraid? A similar pattern is often displayed in human interactions. If I expect people to treat me poorly, they often will, because my demeanor alienates and offends them. Without even realizing it, I stimulate in them their negative behaviors toward me, such as taking advantage of me, rejecting me, or ignoring me. People rarely get walked on except when they're lying on the sidewalk.

Similarly, if I envision tragedy in my life, it will often follow me around. Negative attitudes are like a cloud of doom, distracting us from taking care of our bodies, reducing our attention when we're driving, or making us insensitive to how others are feeling—all of which join with a myriad of similar factors to produce personal disasters. Although we don't realize we're doing it, *we're* predisposing our own fate.

Conversely, if I'm optimistic about life, good things will usually follow. People who smile a lot are liked by others. People who are friendly, make friends. People who aim at success, and work to reach a goal with diligence and creativity, more often than not achieve it.

If there is one truth I've discovered after years of rubbing shoulders with those who've been successful in the corporate world, both in the service and manufacturing industries, it's that they're no smarter than anyone else. They're not even more lucky. Neither were they born, necessarily, with golden spoons in their mouths. They are merely men and women who believe in themselves and who work long, hard hours to succeed—sticking with their dreams long after others have given up. It's usually not brilliance that makes a person a success, but tenacity.

We all like to be around positive, confident people. We help those people along when we can. We hire them. We promote them. We stay with them. And if we want to be successful, we need to emulate them.

Consideration 2: Astrology keeps people from taking the responsibility for their own lives.

The *astrological scam* is not in what it claims, regardless of how well or poorly it performs. *The scam is what you don't do because of it.* Astrology affirms a belief system that removes from us the fundamental *responsibility* for our own lives. Any system that says our lives are ruled by fate, luck, karma, or being in the right place at the right time is extremely dangerous. It encourages in us the idea that we have to take whatever life brings us and just go along with the flow. It turns us from actors to reactors.

More than that, it *dehumanizes* us.

When God said at the creation, "Let us make man in our image" (Genesis 1:26), He was referring, partially at least, to our unique power of choice. Animals don't choose their behavior. They follow instinctive patterns and respond to stimuli in predictable ways. Pavlov's dogs could be trained to salivate on command—but they couldn't design the systems that caused them to salivate or understand *why* they did. Apes can be trained to push in sequence a series of buttons with symbols on them, mimicking speech. But no ape ever faced a moral dilemma or chose to act out of pattern in order to facilitate a long-term objective.

Only humans do that.

When we allow ourselves to be bilked into believing we do not control our own destiny, we give up that which makes us what we are. We fail to behave in a wholly human fashion. And that's a terrible price to pay for a bit of useless advice found next to the funny pages of your newspaper.

Astrology makes us all victims. It tells us we are swept this way and that, due to the accident of our birth, that we are wholly at the mercy of factors beyond our control. If I'm a Leo,

I will behave in this way. If I'm a Virgo, I'll behave in that way. It's bigotry on an astrological scale. I do not master my world. I am mastered. I am a pawn in the great chess game of life.

There is something perverse in the human psyche that makes us susceptible to this line of reasoning. We seem eager to allow others to control our behavior. We take a masochistic pleasure in being dominated. A man says of his wife, "My old lady won't let me out for the night, Charlie. You guys will have to play cards without me." Or a secretary blames her boss for her overworked schedule. "I don't know what I'm going to do! I just have to get this report out for Mr. Brown before three, and I'm so worried." We forget that we don't *have* to do anything. We do what we do because what we receive from acting according to a certain pattern outweighs what we'd lose if we didn't.

When I work late at the office, it's not because I *have* to. I work late because there are things I *want* to get done, things which can have a definite impact on my future. You may feel that there's no difference between being told what you have to do and choosing to do that very same thing. But there's a *world* of difference between the attitudes these alternative approaches create. One makes me a victim; the other makes me responsible.

The type of thinking astrology encourages has a profound impact on our overall psychological health too. A major objective in life, to which each of us should aspire, is to become wholly *functional* human beings. This means we need to escape from the dysfunctional patterns of thinking and acting that we've brought with us from childhood. One aspect of this is our need to go from environmental control to self-control—going from being pushed this way and that by factors which surround us in the outside world, to *choosing* the things we'll believe and making our own decisions about what we'll do.

Few of us realize just how much baggage we bring with us into adulthood. Transactional analysis, a contemporary system for helping people cope with life in responsible ways, says that we all bring with us into adulthood a memory bank filled with thousands of hours of "parent tapes," which far too many of us allow to dominate our adult behavior. Our perceptions of who we are, what we like, and what we ought to do with our lives are all programmed by these parent tapes. We become enmeshed in the expectations of others, never discovering who *we* are or what *we* want out of life.

As a result, we never become really *whole.*

Whether we allow our parent tapes, built out of *how we were raised,* to control our destiny, or accept the astrological claim that our destiny is controlled by *when we were born,* we are being molded into someone else's expectations. And the end result is a demoralization of our incentive to grow. Why labor to become more in control of your own life if your destiny is determined by the stars? Why struggle to make better and better decisions if your course is already set?

The real scam in astrology, and its more mundane counterparts, is what it does to us in our deepest struggles for whole personhood.

Consideration 3: Some Christians use chance methods for making decisions that amount to little more than "baptized" astrological thinking.

While few Christians would readily acknowledge astrology as the wellspring for their perspectives on life, there are some areas where remarkably similar thinking can be seen within Christian congregations. I remember one especially pious friend of mine who used to open his Bible at the beginning of each day, flip through the pages with his eyes closed, and jab his finger down on a passage of Scripture at random. That text was his guide for the day. He felt that God guided his finger to the message he wanted him to consider all during that day.

Had I dared to mention that what he was doing seemed about as useful as reading his horoscope, he would have been deeply offended. After all, he was reading from the *Bible,* wasn't he? Surely God would guide him to the right message in this manner if he asked Him to!

Perhaps so. Yet taking the words of Scripture out of their

context and reading with no thought to what they *mean*, turns them into little more than religious slogans. It reduces us to "bumper-sticker" Christianity, fixing the available insights at the most shallow level possible.

God's Word deserves better treatment.

Had God not given my friend a good mind to use in studying His Word, his dependence on the vagaries of chance or the gusts of wind blowing across the pages of the Bible might have seemed more understandable. But trusting to chance, rather than exerting the energy to "search the Scriptures," seems highly irrational, representing the laziest possible approach to spiritual growth.

None of *us* would be so foolish as to trust our future to chance, of course. Or *would* we?

How many of us ignore the opportunities we have to study God's Word in depth, so that we can really come to know His will, and thus be able to map out a strategy for living that promises continual growth? How many of us really *invest* in our futures? Most of us have Bibles in our homes—probably several on them in various versions. Sometimes we even carry a Bible with us to church. Yet do we use the Bible with all that much more intelligence and commitment than my friend did? Are we *really* students of God's Word? We may look up a text when the Bible teacher or pastor asks us. We may offer a few very generalized observations during a Bible class, having failed to study the lesson. We may congratulate the pastor on his fine sermon, even when we've failed to understand much of what he was saying.

And in all these behaviors we continue to subsist at the shallowest possible level of understanding of God's message to humanity. How different is that from the person who picks up the newspaper each morning to check out his horoscope?

The question could well be asked, Isn't seeking to know God's will in our lives *itself* simply a Christianized version of astrology? Aren't we still handing over the control of our destiny to someone else? I don't think the parallel is at all exact, although the potential is certainly there. Seeking God's will *can* easily deteriorate to the level of reading our horoscope, unless we clearly understand the role *we* must always play in ordering our lives.

The Christian life is *not* a passive experience. We are not pawns on the great celestial chessboard, moved this way and that by Players far beyond our ken. Each of us has the capacity to *act*. We make decisions each day that determine whether we will be part of the problems in our world or part of God's solution. *We* make them.

According to the Bible there is a momentous current in today's world, flowing deliberately toward climactic events. We are all moved along in that current, yet we are not flotsam, pushed along with no volition of our own—as philosophical or religious systems like astrology would have us believe. Instead, we are living beings, each with his own will. We are participants in the flow. There is no "scam" here, astrological or otherwise. We control where we go. We choose our own destiny.

Beyond Astrology to Wholeness

Systems like astrology, natural or "baptized," depend on ignorance. They feed on people's gullibility and lack of sophistication. They take the low self-image so many of us possess and use it against us, to shove us even deeper into the murk of believing we cannot make our lives what we want them to be.

The truth of God's Word, however, is that He values us so highly that He sent His only Son to ransom us from the degradation of sin and reinstate us as His sons and daughters. See John 3:16. God values us more highly than we do ourselves.

The apostle Paul summarizes the standing we hold with God—and should exercise in our daily lives—in these words: "The love of Christ leaves us no choice, when once we have reached the conclusion that one man died for all and therefore all mankind has died. His purpose in dying for all was that men, while still in life, should cease to live for themselves, and should live for him who for their sake died and was raised to life. With us therefore worldly standards have ceased to count in our estimate of any man; even if once they counted in our understanding of Christ, they do so now no longer. When anyone is united to Christ, there is a new world; the old order has gone, and a new order has already begun." 2 Corinthians 5:14-17, NEB.

This new order is both positive and directive. No longer tossed this way and that by the whim of chance, we see ourselves as agents for change, taking an active role in making our world a better place to live. No longer living merely for ourselves, we begin living for a higher purpose—*living* for the same reasons Jesus *died:* to bring hope and salvation to a world.

As whole people, we do not see ourselves as victims of a capricious fate. We laugh at the idea that the stars dictate our future. Our own choices—or lack thereof—determine the quality of our lives.

When we ask God into our lives, requesting that He take control, He comes—but only at our invitation. When we follow His will, obeying His commands, we do so out of *our choice.* We don't *have* to do what God says. We *choose* to do so. We're never in danger of becoming embittered over what we have to give up in order to walk the Christian life, because we don't have to give up anything. There are some things we'll choose to set aside in preference to some others, but all of life involves trade-offs. We give up what we do because we anticipate receiving something far better in return.

The "astrology scam" seeks to rob us of all this. It wants us to give up being sons and daughters of God in favor of being pawns of destiny. It's a bad deal.

Thought Questions:

1. If someone could "prove" to you that astrology *worked,* would that unsettle your faith in God and the gospel? What is the danger in looking at prophetic results, as opposed to biblical truth?
2. Who is responsible for what happens in your life? Are you? Is God? Is Satan? Do you often feel that you are the victim of a fate you cannot control?

3. How important to you is being able to *choose* the path your life takes? Is taking responsibility for your own life contrary to a life of faith?
4. How do you feel about the idea that you are a "pawn" on some celestial chessboard? Is there room in the Christian life for independent decision making, or is everything we do "influenced" by God or Satan?
5. Have you ever felt embittered over what you've had to give up in order to live the Christian life? Where is the "fatal flaw" in this type of attitude? What are the trade-offs you enjoy as a result of being a Christian?

Chapter 7

Spiritualism and Spirituality

The occult elements in astrology are masked by its apparent innocence. This isn't true of some other belief systems, including those we'll consider in the next few chapters. They *feature* the occult, drawing upon the curiosity of the uninitiated to stimulate the interest that serves as the foundation for the sell job.

Many of us, as children, were warned by our Christian parents about the dangers of spiritualism. We were warned not to consult Ouija boards or tamper with the occult. As we've grown up, however, we may not have made the connection between these early admonitions and some of what we see in the modern world around us, masquerading as popular psychology and parapsychology.

Spiritualism has gone uptown.

Numinous. It's a word we don't hear too often in our normal, everyday conversation. *Numinous* refers to the mysterious and supernatural, to that which appeals to the higher emotions or the aesthetic sense. Most commonly, it is used to describe the feeling we get when we're in the presence of divinity, such as when we're praying or experiencing the hand of God in some dramatic, irrefutable way. It's that holy awe we feel when we're very near to God, reminding us how small we are and how vast and otherworldly God is, driving us to our knees, and touching our hearts. It's what the publican felt when, in contrast to the proud Pharisee, he cried out, "God be merciful to me a sinner." Luke 18:13.

It's easy to assume that Christians are the only ones capable of experiencing a sense of the numinous—or of even wanting to. We forget how strong the urge is in every one of us for some type of spiritual experience. Many people today have little clear understanding of what it means to be a spiritual person, yet they crave that sense of immortality or purposefulness which comes from some contact with the numinous. They know something is missing from their lives; they just don't know what it is. People want to believe there is a deeper meaning to their existence, that their lives count for something.

The antimaterialistic, back-to-the-earth movement so popular during the late 60s and early 70s, with its strong spiritual flavor, has lost some of its appeal these days. Yet interest in the spiritual has remained. The hippies have been replaced by the yuppies, yet the interest in finding meaning and purpose in life is just as strong.

Those segments of the religious community which promise strong contact with the numinous on a very personal level, such as the neo-Pentecostals, the fundamentalists, and the various religious cults and sects, are flourishing. Even athletes, who were once ranked among the least spiritual segments of our community, are now public in their expressions of spiritual interest and commitment. It's a little unnerving to hear a boxer who has just knocked his opponent senseless thank God for giving him the opportunity to do so and for being with him during the fight!

The Appeal of Spiritualism

Webster defines *spiritualism* as "the view that spirit is a prime element of reality." This definition shares a common interest with the perspectives of Christians everywhere. We, too, believe that the spirit is a prime element in life. Yet spiritualism is generally understood to involve a whole spectrum of activities relating to contacting the spirits of those who have passed over to "the other side," including nontraditional practices such as seances, Ouija boards, and levitation—none of which classify as "spiritual" in the Christian sense.

Spiritualism has to do with spirits, but not *spirituality*. Still, it would be a mistake to assume that all who practice spiritualistic activities are interested merely in establishing contact with the dead. Some, at least, seek such contact to support their need to believe that there is more to life than the mundane rituals of making a living and surviving from day to day. That they seek this expansion in their lives in nontraditional ways may be tied, at least partially, to a decline in confidence in mainline Christianity. Many of the larger Christian bodies, in particular, are perceived as having lost some of their fervor. People sometimes find religious services so bland that they leave disappointed. Sermons on how to solve family problems or on the political issues of the day have interest as lectures, but they do little to put people in contact with God. Pleasant homilies and sweet poems are inoffensive, but they fail to inspire awe in the face of the omnipotent One.

Spiritualism must be viewed as an alternative to Christian thinking on a broad spectrum of issues, including matters relating to life and death. It needs to be evaluated on its own merits, as a competing system of belief. Specifically, it must be evaluated from the perspective of how well it meets the overall spiritual needs of people. Following are some of the more obvious weaknesses of spiritualism as a belief system.

Weakness 1: Spiritualism substitutes a gospel of knowledge for the biblical gospel of grace.

One of the most difficult concepts for us humans to grasp is the idea that God Himself has *provided* salvation. It is something wholly outside us, irrespective of our response. God has done it not because we asked for it or deserved it, but because He is who He is. Salvation is His free gift to mankind, which we, as individuals, need only accept.

Spiritualism is one of many systems man has designed to find a way of salvation other than this free gift. As with these many others, spiritualism is a way for man to *achieve* salvation rather than *receive* it. And, like most ideas, there is nothing new in spiritualism.

In the early centuries of the Christian church there was a competing belief system that some Christians tried very hard to integrate into orthodox Christianity. Scholars call this belief system *Gnosticism.* Gnostic beliefs were complex, and we can't take the time here to study them in detail, but they essentially involved the idea that there is a secret knowledge about how to be saved that man must discover and follow to escape this dark world and pass into the world of light. Because Gnostics believed there would be a heavenly man sent from God with this secret knowledge, and because it had other beliefs that paralleled Christian teachings in some respects, Gnosticism *seemed* quite close to Christianity—and certain aspects of its teachings began to seep into the church.

Yet Gnosticism *wasn't* Christianity. Far from it. The Gospel of John was written largely to counter this Gnostic theology. When John wrote, "In the beginning was the Word" (John 1:1), he was using terminology that rang true to the Gnostics, who sometimes referred to their heavenly man as "the Word." A common ground was established. But when he concluded, "And the Word was made *flesh,*" (John 1:14) he was cutting at the very root of Gnosticism. Gnosticism was a dualistic system, with contending absolutes of good and evil. The Gnostics believed that the world was inherently evil and that man's spiritual goal was to escape it. Because the world was evil and the heavenly man was good, he couldn't ever really set foot here; he only "appeared" to do so—in phantom form, not in the flesh.

Christianity, repudiating dualism, believes that only God is absolute. In the Christian view, this world is inherently good, with sin only a temporary incursion that God has allowed to run its course and will one day remove.

Modern spiritualists draw much of their inspiration from components of the gnostic belief system—though most modern-day spiritualists probably haven't even heard the word *Gnosticism.* They, too, seek a secret knowledge that comes from "the other side" and feel that this knowledge will in some way help them achieve immortality—an immortality exclusive of God. Like all systems built on human aspiration, spiritualism cannot accept the absolute efficacy of the gospel. Instead, it offers an occult knowledge drawn from the dead, by which we can bypass true spirituality.

It didn't hold water back in biblical times, and it still doesn't now.

Weakness 2: Like other do-it-yourself religions, spiritualism offers a short-cut to spirituality—and like all such short-cuts, it doesn't work.

Spirituality It's an emotion-packed word, isn't it? How does one become more spiritual? And what does becoming more spiritual mean to our relationship with God?

Before we try to answer these questions it's essential that we establish a clear view of how spirituality relates to the gospel The good news of the gospel is that God accepts us just as we are. *There is nothing we can do to make ourselves more attractive to Him than we already are—including becoming more spiritual.* So becoming more spiritual doesn't mean becoming more saved. It doesn't secure God's acceptance.

Then is spiritual growth unimportant? Of course not. As a way of responding to what God has done for us and as a path to greater personal joy and satisfaction, increased spirituality has great value. It's as a route to salvation that spirituality is wholly inadequate.

But how does this relate to spiritualism? Spiritualism exaggerates the importance of spiritual *power* in relationship to faith. It intimates that there is an enhnaced spiritual level to be achieved by establishing contact with "the other side." It claims that there are occult truths to be discovered that will makes us *better* people, more *powerful* people, more *in tune* with the universe.

There is no substance to this expectation. But even if there were, it wouldn't matter. Salvation is not achieved by our accomplishments. It is received because of Jesus' accomplishment for us when He died on the cross.

Sometimes we get very confused over terms like spirituality," and "relationship with God." Exactly what does a relationship with God entail? Is it some sort of mystical closeness we achieve through prayer and fasting, or through beating our bodies until they bleed? Non-Christian religions usually seek the path to increased spirituality along this route. According to these systems, self-denial and self-effacement are critical components, as is the acquisition of supernatural power through initiation into some form of mystery.

This is not the Christian path. The apostle Paul wrote often of the great "battle" we must all wage—a battle to continue trusting God with our lives when the temptation is to take control ourselves. In 1 Timothy 6:12 Paul calls on Christians to "fight the good fight of *faith*" and in 2 Timothy 4:7 he proclaims that he has "fought a good fight" and has *"kept the faith."*

True spirituality is not a matter of spiritual power. It's a matter of learning to trust God with our lives. It comes as a result of "beholding" Jesus in daily Bible study, meeting the crises of life with faith, and learning to live in loving ways by sharing in the Christian fellowship. See 2 Corinthians 3:18. It is a wholly positive path that takes time and the investment of our best energies. We just can't become more spiritual through short-cuts.

Weakness 3: Spiritualism is fundamentally at odds with the biblical views of death and the hereafter—and can't be integrated into the Christian faith.

As will be discussed in greater detail in the next chapter, there are two views on the state of the dead which hold currency within the Christian world today. One says that when we die we go to heaven or hell (or purgatory, in the Roman Catholic view), and the other says that when we die, we die—awaiting resurrection at the second coming of Christ. While these views differ at several important points, *neither* allows for the type of contact with the dead that spiritualism proposes. When a person dies, in the Christian view, his or her involvement in the things of this world ceases.

Spiritualism teaches that there are disembodied "spirits" floating around, like Casper the Friendly Ghost, keeping up with what transpires here on earth and eager to provide a few insights now and then, if they are properly asked. Sometimes, as in the movie *Poltergeist,* these denizens of "the other side" are pictured as being trapped here, playing various forms of mischief until someone comes along to release them from their bondage. At other times they are pictured as wise sages, who have remarkable truths to share with the fortunate individual who achieves contact. Foremost among these "truths" of spiritualism is the idea, best stated by actress Shirley MacLain in her book *Out on a Limb,* that "perhaps our belief in death is the greatest unreality of all."

This all makes interesting fantasy, but it makes poor religion. It is not possible to dabble in spiritualism and be a Christian at the same time. Their contrasting views on all the fundamental issues, including the nature of man's condition at death, are so far apart as to be wholly irreconcilable.

Weakness 4: Spiritualists betray a callous insensitivity when they attempt to bilk people out of their money through playing on their sense of loss.

Séances do not put individuals in contact with the spirits of their departed loved ones. In many cases mediums have proved to be nothing but carnival charlatans grown increasingly sophisticated with modern technology. They're better at it today than they used to be, but what they're doing is as old as human gullibility itself. Magician Danny Korem, for example, has made a career out of exposing the various trickeries employed by supposed parapsychologists and psychics, including such a celebrated individual as Uri Geller. Korem has also had a hand in unmasking other psychic phenomena, such as the Amityville Horror haunted house, which turned out to be an elaborate hoax.

People so desperately *want* to believe that they can share a moment of contact with their departed loved ones that they suspend all objectivity and ignore their critical faculties. They grasp at the feeblest of straws.

Of course, spiritualism doesn't usually *appear* these days in its most crassly commercial aspect. More often it manifests itself in the seductive garb of modern psychology and science, through the specific offerings of parapsychology and transcendental meditation—or as part of the mystical resacralization of the West, through the use of hallucinogenic drugs in the effort to achieve transcendent levels of consciousness. Actress Shirley MacLaine, as an evangelist for the New Age movement, is merely one of the most visible symbols of this renewed interest in the occult in all its forms.

In its cruel misuse of human tragedy, spiritualism is shown to be far less benign than it might seem on the surface. It's not just some archaic belief system, surviving merely as a historical oddity from the turn of the century. In some circles, it's big business. But in all circles it's human manipulation of the least appealing type.

Weakness 5: To the degree that spiritualism isn't just a hoax, it puts people into dangerous contact with the occult world.

We've gone to some lengths to deny the idea that we can contact our departed loved ones through spiritualism, and we've identified the majority of mediums as carnival charlatans. Yet it would be a serious mistake to deny the realities which lie behind the occult phenomena which sometimes occur in association with spiritualistic activities. The apostle Paul wrote, "Our fight is not against any physical enemy: it is against organizations and powers that are spiritual. We are caught up against the unseen power that controls this dark world, and spiritual agents from the very headquarters of evil." Ephesians 6:12, Phillips. There is a serious reality behind certain elements in the occult.

As we've observed, Christianity is not a dualistic religion. We do not believe in two ultimate, coequal principles in the universe—good and evil. We believe everything which exists was created by a loving God. However, we do believe in evil and in the personification of that evil in the form of a personal devil—a fallen spiritual being known variously as Lucifer, Satan, and the devil. And we believe that this being wages a spiritual warfare with God, in which he seeks to involve human beings as pawns. While it is unpopular in these days of skepticism to discuss Satan and his organization of fallen angels—and even some Christians are no longer comfortable with the topic—it is wholly biblical. Satan is not all-powerful, but he is a spiritual being with remarkable powers and a will to use them against God and His people.

While some spiritualist mediums are clever magicians who make a fast buck out of duping gullible people, others are truly in contact with the spirit world—not the spirits of the departed dead but the spirits of demons working miracles. See Revelation 16:13, 14. The claim that this is contact with the dead is merely a mask that gives evil spirits a point of contact with human beings. Those who deny the reality of the devil and his angels and affirm the possibility of speaking personally with the dead have no defense against spiritualism.

It's a dangerous place to be.

Standing at the Brink of Death

Speculations over what happens to a person when he dies all face the common difficulty that there is no empirical evidence to back up whatever opinion we hold. But what about out-of-body experiences—those who claim to have died and come back to life, with tales of their whole lives passing before their eyes and a bright light drawing them away from this world? There are apparent similarities to many of these stories, often involving a great sense of peace that comes over those nearing death. Doesn't this mean they were about to enter heaven?

On the surface, these near-death experiences seem to offer something of substance. But on closer examination this proves untrue. The individuals involved don't know *what* they saw, their stories differ at the level of the specifics, and the mere fact that they were in such terrible physical condition as to have been almost "dying" brings their capabilities as objective analysts under serious question. The physical and emotional trauma they were experiencing was, itself, quite sufficient as an explanation for what they saw or felt.

Obviously, there is no way to disprove such claims. Neither is there any reason to try. When a person nears death, it is entirely understandable that he would experience sensory phenomena that involve religious overtones and exotic manifestations. Most people face death with the deepest of all possible terrors. At such times everything they've heard or read about what people experience at death, along with all the religious programming they've absorbed during a lifetime, comes to the front. It has been demonstrated by modern neurological techniques that we never actually forget anything. We often cannot recall information from the distant past, but it's still encoded in our brain cells. By stimulating certain areas of the brain, researchers have caused subjects to recall events in the most minute detail, even including tastes and smells. Everything we've ever learned is still with us.

It may be that the trauma of a brush with death is sufficient to draw all this up, creating the images and perceptions typical in these near-death narratives.

A Better Way

Spiritualism is viewed by some as nothing more than a vague, curious possibility—something they don't really believe in, but don't mind considering, in a sort of playful, noncommitted manner. The problem with this easy-going, very modern attitude is that it often hinders honest seeking for extremely important answers on life's key questions.

It's important that each of us arrive at some sense of conviction about the spiritual issues of life. We don't want to meander through life in a daze, unwilling to think seriously about who we are, what life is all about, and the meaning of existence—and then face the specter of an imminent death with no answers or the support system those answers provide.

Knowing what happens when a person dies is important only in relation to other matters of spiritual significance. Obviously, we can't influence *what* happens, in any absolute sense. When we die, we die. We can't take anything with us, and we can't argue with the reality of death when it comes. The only thing we can influence is our *preparation* for what happens. The Christian believes that by accepting Jesus and the gift of life He provides, death can be anticipated with great peace of mind, rather than terror.

No element in spiritualism can begin to match the Christian hope. Spiritualism is an empty dream, with many questions but no answers. We each deserve better than that.

Thought Questions:

1. What has been your personal experience with the numinous? When have you felt that holy awe that comes at points of unusual closeness to God? How did it affect you?
2. Why do you think people would want contact with the dead? In your opinion, what is the appeal of spiritualism?
3. Is it enough to *know* what God has revealed about His plan for saving mankind? What does the Christian need beside knowledge in order to enjoy deep spirituality and the hope of eternal life?
4. What can we do to cause God to love us more than He already does? How do we improve our standing with God? Will becoming more spiritual make us more attractive to Him?
5. What would you say are the dangers from the occult? Is the idea of a fallen spiritual being working in an organized manner to subvert the human race one you can apply in your day-to-day life?
6. Where is the key spot in which spiritualism falls down? How is the Christian hope different from the promises of spiritualism?

Chapter 8

The Endless Cycle of Reincarnation

It seems, sometimes, that the oldest ideas continue to be the most pervasive. They take on new shape according to each particular culture, but they continue to prevail. In the marketplace of ideas, reincarnation is "old hat." It's been a key element in religions that have come and gone, as well as in some that continue to be vital today.

Interestingly enough, however, even in our scientific age, reincarnation is once again becoming a "hot item." In the next two chapters we'll consider just how this has taken place, along with some of the specific challenges it offers to the gospel message.

Brooding over the pain of life and the inevitability of death, Job cried out, "If a man die, shall he live again?" Job 14:14.

It's a question that's been asked by virtually every religion from the ancient Hebrews to the latest guru or political utopian. And almost always the answer is a resounding Yes! What differs from religion to religion are the specifics on the shape and meaning of that new life.

The need to feel that there is some form of personal immortality available to each of us runs very deep in all recorded literature throughout the history of mankind, from the *Bhagavad-Gita* to actress Shirley MacLaine's two autobiographical books, *Out on a Limb* and *Dancing in the Light*. Approaches to it differ from culture to culture, but the preoccupation with life after death is almost universal.

Perhaps this is because life is so short. Sometimes it seems that by the time we are mature enough to appreciate it, life is nearly over, and we ask ourselves, "Can this really be the end? Can it be over so soon?" This desire for something more is certainly part of our God-given heritage. God has clearly "set eternity in the hearts of men." Ecclesiastes 3:11, NIV.

The Endless Cycle of Rebirth

Is death the end?

The atheist believes so. To him, man is just an intelligent animal who lives on only in the memories of those who follow. Atheistic science acknowledges a genetic immortality we all have through passing on our heredity to our children, but that's all. There is no room in atheism for personal immortality.

However, the number of true atheists in the history of mankind—even among the scientific community—has been small. None of us is wholly immune to the need to feel that there is more to life than what we see.

Of all the ways man has attempted to define his belief that something within him is immortal, the one which has gained the largest number of adherents down through the years is the cyclical view of rebirths known as *reincarnation.* Reincarnation is a theme that runs deep in both Hinduism and Buddhism and is almost universal in the Orient. It is a recurrent theme in rabbinic literature and flourished in the early Christian church in the form of Gnosticism—a variant theology based on "secret knowledge" that we discussed at some length in an earlier chapter.

In the Orient, the popular expressions for reincarnation are *punar-janman,* "again birth," and *samsara,* "the round of births and deaths." In India, reincarnation is inevitably tied to the idea of *karma,* the belief that we are totally responsible for whatever we do in this life—so responsible, in fact, that even death does not settle our accounts. Indeed, for the Eastern mind, reincarnation becomes a type of bondage in which mankind is trapped, an endless cycle of punishment we can hope to escape only through *nirvana*—which isn't heaven, but rather the ending of the cycle of living hell, when absolute dissolution of the soul is finally earned.

It is important to understand the full implications of reincarnation as taught in the East before we look at how it has been adapted to Western thinking. In the East, reincarnation is not the source of mankind's hope and joy, as is eternal life in Christian theology, but the cause for his bitterest enslavement. When a man dies, he *must* be born again and again and again. He is locked in an endless cycle of rebirth, the hopeless pawn of a cosmic design that cares nothing about compassion and mercy.

A Pervasive Philosophy

Most of us probably don't realize just how deeply belief in reincarnation has penetrated our own culture today, even in this so-called Christian nation. Outside the mainstream of the Christian community there is a widespread acceptance of reincarnation as a plausible answer to questions about the meaning of life and death. According to a 1982 Gallop poll, 23 percent of Americans—one in four—believe in reincarnation. Popular literature, such as Richard Bach's best seller *Jonathan Livingston Seagull* and the whole genre of horror and occult novels, selling millions of volumes each year for authors such as Steven King and Peter Stroud, *assumes* a belief in reincarnation. Popular movies, such as the immensely successful Star Wars saga, incorporate a belief in reincarnation as a fundamental thematic element. Rock musicians write songs about reincarnation, and television often features the reincarnation theme in seemingly innocuous packages, with people coming back to life as cars or animals—or, as in the Lily Tomlin, Steve Martin movie, *All of Me,* as a person of the opposite sex.

Earlier, we referred to Shirley MacLaine and her well-published interest in reincarnation. According to *Time* magazine (September 10, 1984), she is not alone among Hollywood celebrities: "Glenn Ford was a Christian martyr, eaten by a lion. Loretta Lynn was a Cherokee princess and a mistress of one of the King Georges, she is not sure which. Shirley MacLaine and Sylvester Stallone were both beheaded, she by Louis XV, and he during the French Revolution. Stallone thinks he may have been a monkey in Guatemala, and MacLaine is sure she was a prostitute in a previous life. Many Hollywood stars and other celebrities are firm believers in reincarnation. With the aid of mediums and hypnotists, some of whom specialize in regressing people back to the distant past, they have tracked down what they say are some basic facts about previous lives."

Reincarnation is the *in* thing, today. This may be due, in part, to its roots in Eastern mysticism—which most Americans don't fully understand, but many admire nonetheless. There is a craving today for anything that is different. Anything which offers a unique flavor, untainted by what are considered to be the bankrupt ideas of Western society.

Reincarnation aptly fills the bill.

The Power of the Paranormal

There is a wide variety of so-called paranormal experiences which hold credence in popular mythology these days. Tabloids, such as *The National Enquirer, The Star,* and *The National Observer,* splash them in front of our faces at supermarket check-out stands. We listen to people discuss them on television and radio talk shows. They have become so common that we almost take them for granted. They include mystical "out-of-body" excursions (people who've been certified dead but have been resuscitated and went on to tell what they saw when unconscious), and hypnotically induced returns to previous reincarnations—to name only a few.

It's very difficult to argue with someone who says, "I know what I saw," or, "I was there, you weren't." It's like the person who declares with absolute conviction that he has been taken for a ride in a flying saucer. There is no way to *disprove* what he claims.

However, there is also no way to *prove* it.

The issue of reincarnation cannot be proved *or* disproved on the basis of anecdotal information—what people *say* they saw or felt. There are far too many factors, both coincidental and psychological, that influence what people experience and how they *interpret* what they experience. We cannot trust such reports as accurate, objective sources of information. Our relationship to these phenomena must be based on one of two foundations: (1) to the scientist, it must be demonstrated in the laboratory; and (2) to the Christian, it must be evaluated by how consistent reincarnation is with the fundamental tenets of God's revelation, the Bible.

In spite of its broad popular appeal, there are several flaws in the logic of reincarnation. The following list of "problems" isn't intended to be exhaustive, but it does identify some of the key areas of concern and draws a few specific contrasts. In the list, the first issue raised would be significant to anyone with a Western orientation, Christian or not, merely as a feature of an objective evaluation. The issues raised after that are problems reincarnation poses specifically to the Bible-believing Christian.

From the comments which follow, it will be clear that I am persuaded that it's impossible to believe in both the gospel message *and* reincarnation. They are philosophical concepts cut from entirely different cloth—mutually exclusive in their views on all the really key spiritual and ethical issues.

Problem 1: As a system for upgrading the moral fiber of the race, reincarnation isn't working.

A telling argument against reincarnation is to ask, If man is being born over and over in an effort to purify himself, why hasn't the race progressed to some great height of morality after all these centuries? While we are certainly progressing technologically, is mankind any more moral or ethical today? Is a race that has invented the hydrogen bomb and created the death furnaces of Auschwitz more noble than the peasant sheepherders and grain raisers of the agricultural era? Is a punk rocker of the 80s wearing chains and spiked hair, a more refined soul than the harpist on a hill above Athens?

Reincarnationists are unaware of this philosophical weakness in their system, but they argue in response that being born again doesn't necessarily *provide* growth, only the *potential* for growth. That the human race hasn't developed further is a testimony to human failure and to wasted opportunity. We *could* have evolved; we just haven't yet.

But this response doesn't really address the issue. If there is some sort of cosmic design which is utilizing reincarnation as the mechanism for ennobling the human race, it's a failed design.

Problem 2: With its "iron law of karma," reincarnation as an ethical system offers a pale substitute for the gospel.

My two sons are frequently disobedient. I'm told that there are parents who don't see this pattern in their children, and I'm willing to believe it to some degree, having had daughters who were less perverse than my sons. But the fact is the boys are often in trouble. If I were to deal with my sons on the basis of justice alone, they'd hardly have time to take a breath between trips out to the woodshed. But mixed with my justice are heavy doses of mercy. I want the boys to grow up obeying me, of course, but I also want them to love me, and love involves mixing justice and mercy.

That's the way God deals with us.

Reincarnation, however, is an ethical system preoccupied only with justice. The iron law of karma leaves no room for human error or forgiveness. Its demand for perfection is absolute. No mercy is allowed to penetrate. What we do in this life wholly determines our fate. In a sense, the law of karma creates a vast seat of judgment, but places no one on it as Judge. It is a cold, inanimate justice, without compassion—a human-designed alternative to God's revelation, with only one side of the story presented.

The gospel involves justice, too, but it balances justice with mercy. The law of God is every bit as absolute as the law of karma, specifying those behaviors which are and aren't acceptable to a righteous God. But in the gospel picture, God interposes Himself between us and our fate in the person of His Son. As the apostle Paul writes, "The wages of sin is death; but the gift of God is eternal life." Romans 6:23.

Hinduism, one of the great wellsprings for reincarnation, has been termed an anti-life dogma. It proposes cosmic bondage to an eternal law that offers no escape. In its system of rebirths, mankind's only hope is to die. In the gospel, our blessed hope is to *live*.

In the Christian view of the universe, God is a God of love. Sin is wholly out of harmony with His person, and He has committed the whole treasury of heaven to its elimination. God has provided, in the final judgment of the living and the dead, a *solution* to the sin problem in the person of His Son. This is an ethical formulation so opposed to the reincarnationist view that there is no point of common ground.

Problem 3: Reincarnation, as a conceptual model, is wholly at odds with the biblical picture of God's plan for human history.

Simply put, reincarnation is an open-ended system, while Christianity is closed. Reincarnation involves a life cycle that just goes on and on, while Christianity is linear, with a historic flow that is rushing headlong toward a dramatic conclusion.

One of the difficulties in contrasting Christian thinking with the reincarnationist view on what happens when we die is that Christianity itself has absorbed Eastern thought to some degree, muddying the conceptual picture considerably. There are two general Christian viewpoints in circulation today about the state of the dead: (1) the idea that when we die, we go to heaven or hell (or purgatory, in the unique Roman Catholic view), depending on our faith or behavior during the life we've lived; and (2) the idea that when we die, we die, waiting in the grave until Jesus returns to resurrect mankind and execute final judgment.

As a general rule, evangelical Christians have combined

elements from these two views, entertaining at the same time a belief in a last days conclusion to human history as we know it and a belief that when we die we go to heaven or hell, in sort of a "holding pattern" until Jesus returns.

Last-day events (eschatology) is a fascinating topic for speculation. Everybody who believes in the return of Jesus seems to have his or her own viewpoint on exactly how it's all going to happen. Theological jargon, such as premillennialism, postmillennialism, and dispensationalism is tossed around, and there is a great interest in charts and tables which outline the proposed events in a neatly organized sequence. While there are significant differences in the detailed listing of events, there is one bedrock concept in all Christian eschatology: a belief that in the last days God will deal, once and for all, with the sin question. When Jesus comes back, the parenthesis of sin will be closed. Human history in a world of sin will be ended with a resounding period.

Reincarnation, on the contrary, feeds on the idea that things have always been as they now are and will always continue in the same path. Under the reincarnationist scheme, if we're good enough, perhaps we'll progress a little with each rebirth, but chances are that we'll mess up somewhere along the line and get set back a few births. Regardless of what happens to us, however, the cycle itself continues.

In this, Christianity and reincarnation are wholly at odds.

Problem 4: Modern reincarnationists are attempting a hopeless task in their efforts to extract an Eastern theological concept from its roots and apply it to our Western world.

Modern-day reincarnationists like the idea of having lived previous lives. It appeals to their fantasies of immortality, glory, and self-importance—particularly if they can claim a previous life of heroic proportions. But they would like to extract this aspect of Eastern thought from its milieu, while dropping away the rest—including specifically the precise cause-and-effect enslavement to the law of karma.

But it just doesn't work that way. It would be like trying to present the gospel of salvation in Jesus Christ without Jesus. Without the cross, there is no salvation. And without a *cause* for the cycle of rebirth (the law of karma), there is no cycle.

One of the most prevalent of these modern approaches is what has been called the New Age movement, which we'll consider in some detail in the next chapter. It asserts that we are all gods; we have lived before and will live again; there is no death; and each of us creates his own reality. With this cluster of ideas, New Age establishes itself as a form of syncretic pantheism, drawing its teachings from a wide variety of sources and attempting to create a religion that clings together with bailing wire, featuring tired, worn-out ideas that simply don't fit together.

While it's true that as historical forces *both* Christianity and reincarnation emerged from the East, they are vastly different in thrust, representing viewpoints which have been in conflict for thousands of years—perhaps going all the way back to the Garden of Eden. When the serpent denied Eve's belief that if she ate of the forbidden fruit she would die, offering her an immortality separate from the one God offered, the seeds of today's conflict were planted. Reincarnation springs from an essentially anti-God, anti-life world view and simply cannot be fit into the pro-God, pro-life perspectives of Jesus Christ.

Contrast With Biblical Christianity

The broad areas of contrast between biblical Christianity and reincarnation make them totally incompatible as ethical and religious systems. Jesus said of His message, "You will know the truth, and the truth will set you free." John 8:32, NIV. Christianity is a message of liberation. Reincarnation, on the other hand, offers only imprisonment within the endless cycle of rebirth.

What makes reincarnation attractive is its promise that death is not the end. As we saw earlier, this is a promise with broad appeal. Christianity, too, offers this promise.

The difference is that with the hope of immortality Christianity offers something even better—the promise of *eternal* life. Eternal life, as opposed to mere immortal life, promises a *quality* of life totally different in character from the endless cycle of lives and deaths offered in reincarnation. The Christian hope is not just life that goes on and on, but life filled with meaning and overflowing with joy; life spent with a loving God, rather than running from a cold, passionless law of karma.

"If a man die, shall he live again?" Yes, he may, But not in bondage. In Jesus, we may all live freely and fully, as the children of God.

Thought Questions:

1. Is reincarnation, under the iron law of karma, a promise of hope? How has it become a form of bondage to millions?
2. If reincarnation is, indeed, a cosmic design that leads to increasingly higher levels of ethical stature, where is the evidence of moral improvement in the world today? Are the areas of the world where belief in reincarnation flourishes standard-bearers of ethical evolution?
3. What are the dangers from an ethical system preoccupied with justice alone? What other element is required?
4. Can you integrate the endless cycles of rebirth described in reincarnation into the biblical concept of an end to human history with the second coming of Christ? Is the difference important in your attitude toward God and His people here on Earth?
5. In your opinion, what are the key differences between the concept of immortality and the concept of eternal life? Would these differences impact on how you live your life?

Chapter 9

The New Age Movement

Like many other systems we've reviewed—or might review, if space allowed—the New Age movement has its popular face and its not so clearly understood philosophical underpinnings. Even within the church, New Age teachings surface from time to time, usually presented by well-meaning individuals who don't understand the source of the revolutionary ideas they've stumbled across. It is usually the case that such well-intentioned proponents are knowingly or unknowingly seeking to extract useful psychological or philosophical points of view from the larger New Age milieu. They are merely trying to find ways to help people live happier, more-successful lives.

No one could fault the intent.

It is true there are some interesting ideas to be gleaned from the New Age. Concepts like the "Power of Positive Thinking," from Norman Vincent Peale, and "Possibility Thinking" from Robert Schuller, have had considerable positive impact, helping people to more fully realize their potential. That some critics have grouped them as elements of what we might call "baptized" New Age beliefs doesn't necessarily limit their usefulness.

There are also other individuals, less famous than those named, who from time to time offer seminars to various church groups based on concepts gleaned from New Age ideas. These seminars often offer helpful suggestions in the areas of popular psychology—getting the most from one's abilities, visualizing objectives, and such. Again, the *intent* is positive, and much of the material presented is useful.

The problem with all this, of course, is that it's difficult to know where the good leaves off and the dangerous begins.

The Age of Enlightenment

The New Age views itself as the onset of enlightenment. It sees itself as a syncretism of the best ideas from the past into a totally new and better formula. New Age proponents see their system signaling the passing of the old and the arrival of the new, bringing to human history, for the first time, a comprehensive world view.

It's a bold claim. The question Christians must ask, however, is whether this new syncretism really adds all that much light—or whether it just organizes the various forms of darkness already on the scene.

If you've stayed with me this far into the book, I would expect that you've begun to sense some similar threads woven into the approaches of all the "exotic beliefs" we've considered. You should sense by now that I feel there are some common elements they all share, some common questions we need to ask these systems, and some common flaws to note in the answers they give.

In truth, there is very little in our world that is new. All the systems we humans design reflect our characteristic inclinations. They show the same weaknesses, the same aspirations, and stem from the same common needs. At the root of most of the theological error we see, regardless of how "exotic" it may appear, is the same pattern: mankind attempting to find a way to *earn* the salvation God offers freely.

Why is this bad?

Don't misunderstand the issue. God is not being petty with mankind, stating the outlines for salvation and then declaring, "Do it *my* way or not at all." I think this is the picture we've sometimes painted, but God deserves better of us. The problem with man trying to earn his way into God's favor lies ultimately in its futility. Seeking ways of reaching God or discovering some form of transcendence independent of what God offers freely leads men and women down paths that offer no hope of satisfying the very honest needs they feel. And it also puts off—sometimes permanently—the time when they will respond in a positive way to all that God has done in His offer of salvation. The issues involved are extremely important. Indeed, they are matters of life and death. God is offering eternal life to all—but not all know how to accept it.

Anything that befuddles the mind and leads away from the promptings of the Holy Spirit is bad—because the price can be eternally high.

The New Age movement is in some ways an attempt to consolidate all truth into one vast synthesis. It picks and chooses from some of the most exotic of the ideas we've examined (plus a few we haven't) and brings them all together in new packaging that includes biofeedback, self-hypnosis, yoga, ESP, Jungian dream analysis, Silva Mind Control, primal therapy, shamanistic rituals, reincarnation, spiritualism, Gnosticism, the occult—along with some of the more exotic components of contemporary Christianity. As Shirley MacLaine observes in her book *Out on a Limb*, "What had taken my real attention in the vast volume of material available for study was the fact that so much of the message seemed to be universal—that is, entities channeling through a variety of people in many countries in different languages were saying basically the same thing: Look into yourselves, explore yourselves, you are the Universe."

The New Age can be summed up as the belief that we are all gods, we have all lived before and will live again, there is no death, and each of us creates his or her own reality. In one way or another we've touched on several of these themes in virtually every exotic belief we've considered. The New Age merely brings them all together in one eclectic system.

A Successor to Christianity

What do the words "new age" mean? Essentially, "new age" must be understood as a contrast with the "old age" of Christianity and rationalism. It is viewed by its adherents as the inevitable successor to Christianity, as a source of transcendence in this age when the old faiths are collapsing.

Of all the systems we've considered, the New Age is in some ways the most threatening. Like the Russian leader who declared that he was going to bury America, the New Age plans to usurp Christianity. It views the very ideas and ethical principles of Western society as outdated and no longer viable for the modern age.

Of course, simply because the New Age asserts this doesn't make it true. The ideas of the New Age must themselves be analyzed and evaluated. Is it, indeed, more in tune with the basic needs of humanity? Does it provide better answers to the key issues of life?

In the pages that follow I will summarize several major objections to the New Age movement that every thinking Christian needs to consider seriously.*

Objection 1: The New Age believes that everything in the universe is interrelated.

This belief is known in the world of philosophy as *monism.* It asserts that at the fundamental level there is no difference between God, human beings, animals, or inanimate objects. Everything is really the same thing, sharing the same essence. It is to philosophy what the search for a unified field theory is to the world of physics—an attempt to find the fundamental character that all forms of matter and energy share.

Like the search for a unified field theory, the quest for New Age truth faces one key difficulty: The one "Something" that lies behind all we see isn't a principle or an organization of matter and energy. It's a personal God, who is both undefined and undefinable.

---

* In his book, *Unmasking the New Age,* Douglas Groothuis provides a full discussion of these critical points.

Objection 2: The New Age believes that God is in everything.

This concept is technically known as *pantheism.* It has been attractive to various individuals over the centuries, but has never really prevailed for any length of time or captured a wide following. While pantheism appears on the surface to provide viable answers to some of the basic questions about existence, its answers are spiritually bankrupt. They don't satisfy man's longing for a personal God.

Christians have sometimes been confused over pantheism, finding it difficult to draw the line between the Christian view of an immanent God and the pantheistic view of God in everything. Christians believe that God made the universe and upholds it by His power. Pantheism asserts this too, but it doesn't stop there. Pantheism *identifies* God and nature, turning God into nothing more than a force, an essence, or an energy form.

The New Age offers a rather complex "neopantheism," utilizing high-sounding psychological and philosophical language that is really nothing more than window dressing on the same idea. It eliminates wholly the division between the Creator and the created, and in one fell swoop denies the veracity of such "old age" ideas as faith, virtue, and worship.

Objection 3: The New Age believes humanity is God.

While we may not realize it, according to New Age thinking, each of us is a god in disguise. The potential for divinity lies within each person, only waiting for an opportunity to be unleashed.

This is a subtle belief, usually put in the most positive light—challenging us to become all that we can be. Who could deny the value of each person striving to maximize his or her potentials?

The problem is, at its root this view results in the denial of God as a separate, transcendant being whose love brought the universe into existence. On closer examination, we can see it for what it really is—an updated version of Lucifer's aspiration in the very courts of heaven, and his offer to Adam and Eve in the Garden of Eden when he taunted them with the forbidden fruit, saying, "God knows that as soon as you eat it, your eyes will be opened and you will be like gods knowing good and evil." Genesis 3:5, NEB.

When man seeks to usurp the role of God, placing himself on the Eternal Throne, he cuts the very lifeline that connects him with the loving Father. By making himself god, he leaves no room for the true God.

Objection 4: The New Age believes that we all need a change of consciousness.

Like Gnosticism, the New Age denies the rationality of Western thinking. It calls for a raising of our consciousness, by which we'll discover our true identity and enter into a "secret knowledge" that will save us. It advocates the use of whatever techniques or substances are necessary to enable man to escape the limitations of this present life and experience a higher level of consciousness.

There is a fundamentally negative thrust in this suggestion. It denies both the reality we see in the world around us and the objective revelation of God in the Bible. The aspiration for deeper spirituality is a noble one, but Christian spirituality is not tied to "mysteries." God has revealed Himself in the simplest and clearest of language. We do not require initiation into the vagaries of the occult to discover God. He made Himself *man* and dwelt among us.

The New Age is an essentially elitist doctrine, separating those who've had their consciousness raised from the rest of humanity. It depicts a god of the intelligent and sophisticated, who cares little for the ordinary person. And in this it stands on different ground from the gospel, which depicts God as the God of all mankind.

Objection 5: The New Age believes that all religions are one.

This, too, is an old idea, known in theological circles as *syncretism*. It suggests that there are many paths to the truth, with all religions aiming at helping human beings become united with the one.

This sounds generous on the surface. But again, the *one* in this context is not God, but the united mind of mankind. The reason all religions are one in the New Age perspective is that the system has been modeled on man, not on God's revelation. A broad common ground is established by stripping religion of its content.

If all religion was merely man's various forms of aspiration toward the numinous (as the New Age believes), then breaking down the walls that divide religions would be a positive approach. But the Christian religion is not man's aspiration. It is God's revelation.

When one sees the gospel as God's message of love to His wayward children, the New Age approach is shown for what it really is—a repudiation of God Himself.

Objection 6: The New Age believes that mankind can direct his own evolution.

This is a key aspect of where the "new age" in the New Age movement comes from. It believes we are on the edge of a global transformation, when humanity will finally come into its own. All that we know is to be transformed. A better world is a-coming.

Christians also believe in a coming change in the world, but we believe it will be ushered in by the return of Jesus, not the evolving mind of man. Our great hope is not in human evolution, but spiritual revolution, when God comes to make all things new.

Spiritual Futurism: A Reaction to Anemic Spirituality

While the New Age movement is a fairly recent phenomenon and most of us probably don't know a great deal about it, it is gradually moving into the "big time" idea marketplace. New Age thinking is becoming increasingly pervasive, especially among thought leaders and more creative individuals. It deserves our attention.

The reason we might well call the New Age movement "spiritual futurism" is that it attempts to draw together all the various threads of spiritual and religious thinking of past ages, taking the best from each and adding to the mix the disciplines of modern psychological and parapsychological techniques to design a new religion appropriate for the new future it envisions.

The New Age tries to find a sense of the numinous that can be expressed meaningfully in our postindustrial society, with its rapid pace and frenetic style. It's a religion for the 80s and 90s, full of eagerness and expectation. And, like the punk rockers who dance to their own music on the streetcorners, it stands in open repudiation of the historical values and beliefs of the Judeo-Christian tradition.

But it would be a mistake to assume that the New Age emerged in a vacuum, the wild creation of a few bizzare nonconformists. At its root, the New Age is a reaction to the anemic spirituality too often displayed among professed Christians, a condition which has also opened the door to the rampant secularity that pervades our society today. Earlier in the book we quoted sociologists Stark and Bainbridge, and that reference deserves a repeat presentation: "What organizational secularization has produced is a large population of unchurched people who retain their acceptance of the existence of the supernatural. They seem only to have lost their faith in the ability of the conventional churches to interpret and serve their belief in the supernatural."

The New Age is, above all else, a response to a Christian world preoccupied with everything but the gospel. It's one more attempt by lost, confused men and women to discover on their own what we've had all along, but have neglected to share: the good news of a loving God who has made every provision for our joyous future.

Tearing Down the Old Rugged Cross

The major flaw in the New Age is that it tries to offer a salvation for the human race that doesn't include redemption. It seeks to replace the cross with an evolutionary chart. It is mankind pulling himself up by his bootstraps on the very grandest scale. And in the final analysis, this just doesn't work. We can be as articulate and sophisticated as we like, but none of it will save us. When all is said and done, the cause-and-effect relationships that have produced the problems we face in the world today are not based, as the New Age suggests, on human ignorance. Neither can they be solved by increased education or enlightenment, whether philosophical, psychological, or occult.

The problem in this world is sin. And the solution is the redemption offered by Calvary. The New Age is a masterful orchestration of all the various themes of human insight and expression down through the ages. It is a remarkable syncretism. It has many things going for it and only one going against it.

It's just wrong.

The True Religion for the Coming Age

Thousands of years ago the prophets foretold the coming of a "new age," a time when all the problems of this life would be behind us. A time when all the ugliness within the human soul would be cleansed. A time when the lion would lie down with the lamb.

As John the Revelator put it: "I saw a new heaven and a new earth, for the first heaven and the first earth had vanished, and there was no longer any sea. I saw the holy city, new Jerusalem, coming down out of heaven from God, made ready like a bride adorned for her husband. I heard a loud voice proclaiming from the throne: 'Now at last God has his dwelling among men! He will dwell among them and they shall be his people, and God himself will be with them. He will wipe every tear from their eyes; there shall be an end of death, and to mourning and crying and pain; for the old order has passed away!' " Revelation 21:1-4, NEB.

The success of the New Age movement lies in the fact that it promises what mankind wants and needs. Its failure is that it cannot provide what it promises. Only God can do that.

Thought Questions:

1. Do you believe God is in everything? To what degree *does* His presence penetrate His creation?
2. What's wrong with man aspiring to become like God? How does the desire to grow in character relate to the desire to acquire increasing power?
3. How important is the idea of a personal God in your life? Would it matter to you if God were merely a "cosmic force that permeates the universe"?
4. Is Christianity, in your view, out of date? Do we need a new religion for our new, technological world? If you were to design a new religion, what shape would it take?
5. If mankind were to become more intelligent, able to expand his mental capacities far beyond what is now possible, would a point come when he would no longer need God?
6. What is the true "new age?" Are you coming to trust God more fully with your life, in anticipation of that new world?

Conclusion

"Jesus loves me, this I know, for the Bible tells me so." It all comes down to this simple, childlike faith. The various exotic belief systems we've touched on in the previous pages aren't the machinations of bad people. They are the confused thrusting around by men and women who want to believe that there is more to life than what meets the eye. People made by a loving God to live in relationship with Him, but who find themselves cut adrift.

Many of the books written by Christian authors to deal with the dangers posed by competing belief systems settle for making those dangers utterly clear. They focus on where the errors are and how careful we must all be not to fall into them.

I'm persuaded that's not enough.

As Christians, we need to make absolutely sure that we have a firm grasp on the pure, simple gospel. Whatever denomination, sect, or cult we may be a part of, we must be sure that our involvement doesn't confuse our perception of this basic truth about God. And then we must be accessible to a world needing to know that truth.

Above all else, we must not look down our noses at those who don't know the gospel, trusting to the security of our own faith. Faith has a way of drying up when not shared. Clarity of understanding has a way of becoming muddled when not frequently expressed. We don't need to be offensive in our proclamation. We don't need to twist people's arms. What we need is to be *real.* We need to allow our internal conceptualization to express itself in outward behaviors that display faith, hope, and love. When we do this, even the most exotic belief systems in the world will be shown for what they are: pale imitators of the gospel.

"Straight thinking" leads to straight doing. There is an intimate relationship between what we believe and how we act toward one another. I happen to be persuaded that when we live and breathe the generosity of spirit displayed in God's remarkable act of forgiveness which we so often term the "good news," we will be raised from the miasma of confusion and despair that floods the world.

As the songwriter put it, "What the world needs now is love, sweet love." And that, my friend, is what God has to offer—in incredible abundance.

Date Due
